Bertha P. Dutton is a distinguished anthropologist and expert on the archaeology and ethnology of Southwestern and Meso-American Indians. Among her many publications are *Sun Father's Way, The Pueblo Indian World* (with E. L. Hewett), *Happy People: The Huichol Indians,* and numerous journal articles and reviews.

Her work in the field has included research projects and excavations throughout the Southwest and expeditions to Peru, Bolivia, Ecuador, Panama, Guatemala, and Mexico, as well as attendance at conferences in South America, Europe, and the Orient.

The New Mexico Press Women presented to Dr. Dutton in 1971 the coveted Zía award for outstanding publications, and in 1974 she was appointed New Mexico representative to the National Park Service's Southwest Regional advisory committee by Secretary of the Interior Rogers C. B. Morton. She is a Research Associate of the Museum of New Mexico in Santa Fe; for a decade she served as Director of the Museum of Navaho Ceremonial Art, Inc., in that city.

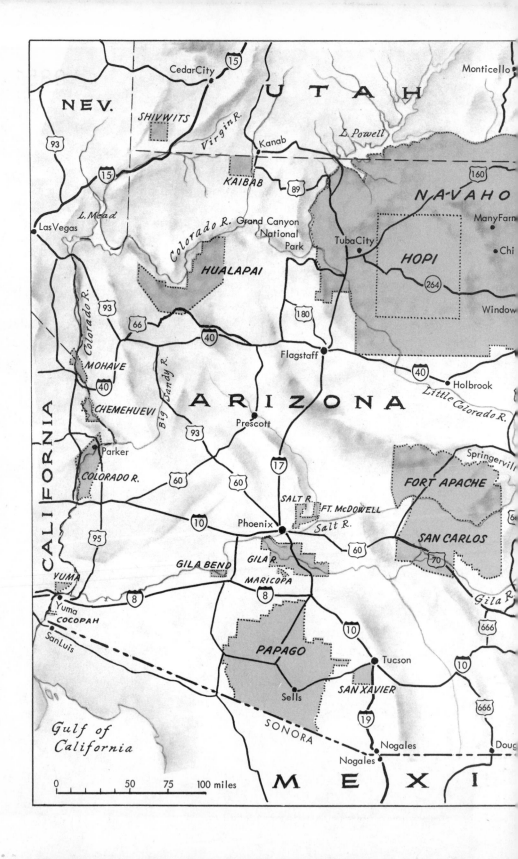

MAJOR INDIAN RESERVATIONS OF THE SOUTHWEST

This book and its two companion volumes,
The Pueblos and *The Ranchería, Ute, and Southern
Paiute Peoples,* were originally published in
one hardcover edition as *Indians of the American
Southwest* (Prentice-Hall, 1975).

Navahos and Apaches:
the Athabascan peoples

Bertha P. Dutton

PRENTICE-HALL, INC.   A SPECTRUM BOOK   ENGLEWOOD CLIFFS, NEW JERSEY

Library of Congress Cataloging in Publication Data

DUTTON, BERTHA PAULINE (date)
    Navahos and Apaches.

    (A Spectrum Book)
    Originally published as chapter 3, The Athabascans, of
the author's Indians of the American Southwest.
    Bibliography: p.
    1. Navaho Indians. 2. Apache Indians. I. Title.
E99.N3D78 1976   301.45'19'7079   76-13555
ISBN 0-13-610832-6

Cover photography: A Navaho sandpainting (Photo by Michael Herion)

Drawing, page 1: An Apache Gáhan dancer's headdress (Museum of the
   American Indian, Heye Foundation, MPA Cat. No. 66-11)

Printed in the United States of America.

10 9 8 7 6 5 4 3 2 1

Prentice-Hall International, Inc., *London*

Prentice-Hall of Australia Pty, Ltd., *Sydney*

Prentice-Hall of Canada, Ltd., *Toronto*

Prentice-Hall of India Private, Limited, *New Delhi*

Prentice-Hall of Japan, Inc., *Tokyo*

Prentice-Hall of Southeast Asia Pte., Ltd., *Singapore*

········· CONTENTS

This book
is respectfully dedicated
to
THE PEOPLE
. . . the original inhabitants
who revered this land
and its creatures
and strived to save and protect them

.........PREFACE

The objective is to make this book generally readable for students, teachers, and travelers who desire knowledge, understanding, and authoritative information regarding the Southwestern Indians; it is for those who wish to know the basic features of Indian life, but who do not, perhaps, have the time or specialized training to read extensively of these various peoples.

"The changing Indian" is much more than an often heard phrase these days. The *changing Indian* is a fact, an almost incomprehensible fact. And changes are occurring at such a rapid pace that whatever one writes may well be out of date before the words are printed. Thus it can be said that this publication is already outdated in certain respects. However, the decade census of 1970 afforded a pivotal point, and the statements made regarding the Indian groups of the Southwest are comparable as of that time.

Throughout this work obvious changes are mentioned, and some of the more covert ones are noted. Although these may vary in kind and extent with the different Indian peoples, certain features in particular are undergoing alterations and transformations: education, living conditions locally and away from the home bases; labor opportunities, industries, economic exploitation, road works, soil treatments, dams and irrigation; health, welfare and social security; old ceremonies and new religions; and in some instances reappraisal of cultural values, appreciation of old mores, and intensification of self-esteem.

The writer has chosen diverse ways of presenting the information assembled; the material is too exhaustive for a book of this scope to be complete. Emphasis has been given to certain aspects of one culture, outstanding facets of another; some of the main features of specific organizations have been portrayed, and the complex and far-reaching traits of the Southwestern societies indicated.

No attempt is made to give equal attention to each and every cultural group. Rather, the design is to show that all of the aboriginal peoples fitted themselves to their particular environment and strove to live harmoniously with nature. To all, the land was sacred. An eminent place was given to the mountains and hills, to the water sources and streams; to the plant and animal life; to the sky above and the celestial bodies seen traversing it, and to the clouds that brought summer rains and winter snows. The individual and the group were linked unconsciously with their surroundings.

And thanks were rendered for the orderly progression of season after season and for the blessings received.

The very way of life itself gave rise to keen observations, philosophical thinking; myths, poetry, song, and drama, which treat of simple things or the majestic; grief and joy, lullabies and love, with diversity of melody and of text. Each of these merits studies by itself. Some of the poetic contributions of the Indians are included, and of non-Indians who have been inspired by them. Something of the philosophy, drama, and other manifestations of Southwestern Indian life will be found in the following pages.

Not infrequently, secondary sources are cited as well as original works. These may be available to readers who wish to pursue studies regarding the Indians; and many will refer to primary works not included with the references mentioned.

It is hoped that reading this book will aid in an appreciation of the first Americans and of their intelligent responses to the surroundings; of their developments and attainments; and then of their tenacious attempts to continue living according to their philosophy and judicious practices in the face of white colonization, conquest, and alternating procedures of the Europeans whose aggressiveness, missionizing and political ambitions, and material desires were so foreign to the Indian beliefs of proper conduct and rewards.

Simply recording brief facts of history and taking note of modern conditions—some of which evidence accretions and others diminutions—have made the consistency of pattern apparent and impressive: peoples came from Asia, slowly populated the Southwest (as well as all of the New World), adopted ways of life in keeping with the conditions at hand, and developed social organizations thus dictated, recognized the limits of their domain and the rights of others, and achieved their respective cultural patterns. Then came the outsiders.

Every conceivable means has been employed to overcome the indigenous peoples and their mores, to make them conform to the white man's way of life. Through four and a half centuries, these efforts have met with relatively little success. Indians may be made to dress like Anglos, eat their foods, dwell in their types of structures, adopt their means of transportation, follow their prescribed curriculums and business methods, undergo the missionizing endeavors of various sects, practice non-Indian forms of government, and the like, but no individual or no aggregate body whatsoever can make the Indian be different from what he *is*. He may change—if he sees fit—or he may mask his feelings and appear to accept the Anglo customs; but the circumstances which produced the people that came to be called American Indians and the centuries that afforded them time to develop a racial identity and distinctive social patterns made an immutable imprint.

Regardless of outside pressures the Indians have remained Indians, and they always will. It appears inevitable that their resolute spirit will bear fruit, now that their numbers are increasing; that their pride in the accomplishments of their people has been intensified; and that they are beginning to discern their existent capabilities and power, and their rights.

ACKNOWLEDGMENTS   The preparation of this publication has extended over a number of years. Much of the research and writing was done during 1971. After that period no further research was pursued. However, as certain individuals undertook the reading of the manuscript several months transpired between its completion and submission to the press. Suggestions of the readers were incorporated: these include later information on occasion, and the addition of certain references and bibliographic items.

As this work took shape, I began to realize how much I owe to the mentors with whom I have been privileged to study, to many Indian friends who have guided my research and added to the knowledge and understanding of their cultures, to my anthropology associates and those in related professions, and to the institutions and foundations that have provided funds for travel and research opportunities and have printed my contributions.

I am most appreciative of the fact that several busy people have taken time to read this manuscript critically and offer advice for its betterment. Among these I give special thanks to C. Fayne Porter, teacher supervisor in language arts at the Institute of American Indian Arts in Santa Fe, who is also a well-recognized author of numerous published works. To teachers in the same school, I likewise give thanks: Michael H. Clark and Paul W. Masters. Colleagues in my profession who have been particularly helpful are Robert C. Euler, Grand Canyon National Park, Arizona; A. E. Dittert, Jr., professor of anthropology, Arizona State University, Tempe, Arizona; John Martin, associate professor of anthropology at the same institution; and Dorothy L. Keur, former professor of anthropology, Hunter College, New York. Although they have not read the manuscript, these colleagues have been very helpful:

Bernard L. Fontana, professor of ethnology, University of Arizona, Tucson; David M Brugge, Curator, Navajo Lands Group, National Park Service, Chaco Center, Albuquerque; and Robert W. Young, student and teacher of Navaho culture.

Within the Bureau of Indian Affairs and the National Park Service, many persons and divisions have supplied information by means of correspondence, telephone calls, printed matter and photographs. Those to whom I render special credits are: Charles R. Whitfield, agency land operations officer, Papago Indian Agency, Sells, Arizona; Kendall Cumming, superintendent, Pima Agency, Sacaton, Arizona; William S. King, superintendent, Salt River Agency, Scottsdale, Arizona; Stanley Lyman, superintendent, Uintah and Ouray Agency, Fort Duchesne, Utah; Espeedie G. Ruiz, superintendent, Ute Mountain Ute Agency, Towaoc, Colorado; José A. Zuñi, superintendent, Hopi Indian Agency, Keams Canyon, Arizona.*

Other persons to whom I am most grateful are Al Packard, whose wide knowledge of Indian arts and crafts has been drawn upon extensively; William Brandon, writer, who has supplied several pertinent articles which otherwise might have been overlooked; Lloyd New, director of the Institute of American Indian Arts, who has furnished information and publications; and Constance (Mrs. William A.) Darkey, Edith (Mrs. William D.) Powell, and Dr. Caroline B. Olin, who have given editorial aid.

For supplying source materials and miscellaneous data, I wish to thank the Navajo Census Office, the Northern and Southern Pueblos agencies respectively, the Jicarilla and Mescalero Apache agencies, the Hopi Tribe, the Zuñi Tribal Council, the Northern Pueblos Enterprises, and many other contributors.

To Fermor S. Church, I owe an especially great debt. Without him this publication would not have been undertaken and completed. His training in engineering (degree from Harvard University) and extensive knowledge of the greater Southwest, its peoples, and its problems—which results from years of teaching at Los Alamos, Santa Barbara, and Taos; from managing the Philmont Boy Scout Ranch; serving in high positions with electrical cooperatives for over two score years; and publishing scientific articles—complemented my learning and experience. Our discussions of matters about which I was writing and manner of presenting them added much to the significance of this undertaking. Some of the maps were prepared

---

*Location of individuals at time of supplying information.

by him: the majority are by Phyllis Hughes of the Museum of New Mexico staff.

As author of *Indians of the American Southwest,* I have drawn on many sources and have quoted material extensively. Permission to quote direct statements was sought, and outstanding cooperation received. Sincere appreciation is expressed to the following authors and publishers:

American Anthropologist, American Anthropological Association, Washington, D. C.

American Antiquity, Society for American Archaeology, Washington, D. C.

American Folklore Society, New York

Arizona Highways, Phoenix

The Arizona Republic, Phoenix

The Caxton Printers, Caldwell, Idaho

Columbia University Press, New York (through a daughter of William Whitman III, Mrs. Philip T. Cate, Santa Fe)

Diné Baa-Hane, Fort Defiance, Ariz.

Frontier Heritage Press, San Diego, Calif.

Indian Tribal Series, Phoenix

Institute of American Indian Arts, Santa Fe

Museum of the American Indian, Heye Foundation, New York

Museum of New Mexico, Santa Fe

Museum of Northern Arizona, Flagstaff

The New York Times

The Progressive, Madison, Wis.

Southwest Parks and Monuments Association, Globe, Ariz.

Southwest Printers, Yuma, Ariz.

Time: the weekly newsmagazine, New York

The University of Arizona (Dept. of Anthropology), Tucson

The University of Arizona (vice-president for business affairs and treasurer), Tucson

The University of Chicago Press, Chicago

The University of New Mexico Press, Albuquerque

University of Oklahoma Press, Norman

University of Washington Press, Seattle

Robert W. Young and *The Gallup Independent,* Gallup, New Mexico

Specific citations are given with the references and full data appear in the bibliography.

To those who contributed their photographic works I am deeply indebted, including the renowned Laura Gilpin, of widespread fame, and Elita Wilson, who has produced outstanding records of the Southwest and its Indian peoples. These, and most of the other contributors, gave their photographs gratis for use in this publication; in other instances museums and other agencies made their contributions without charge. The name of each photographer or source appears with the pictures.

Grateful appreciation is acknowledged to those who typed the final manuscript copy of this work from the rough drafts submitted:

Mary Jean (Mrs. Edward S.) Cook, Rebecca Brown, and Sharyn (Mrs. Kimball R.) Udall.

LINGUISTIC NOTES   In pronouncing Indian and Spanish words, *a* is soft as in "father," *e* as in "grey," *i* as in "machine," *o* as in "whole"; no silent vowels occur. The consonant *h* is silent; *ch* is sounded as in "church"; *j* is like *h* in "hay." In *ll*, the first *l* is lightly sounded and the second takes a *y* sound; thus *Jicarilla* is Heek-ah-REEL-yah.

As noted by a recognized linguist who has worked on Southwestern languages for many years, Professor George L. Trager, "It is customary to refer to a people by the same form for singular and plural (as 'the Hopi,' 'a Hopi,' etc.)."

As with the spelling of the term *Navaho,* some writers follow the Spanish use of "j," though the word is not Spanish, while the modern trend is to use the English "h."

Santa Fe, New Mexico   *Bertha P. Dutton*

Navahos and Apaches: the Athabascan peoples

Long, long after the original, and successive, peoples began to inhabit the western hemisphere and scattered over the two continents, other migrants started to trek from Asia into the New World. Looking to their advent here, perhaps around three thousand years ago, (Young 1968:3) it is found that family groups or small bands of people began coming from northernmost Asia via the Bering Strait. The major body, designated by linguists as the *Nadene*, includes subfamilies called Tlingit, Eyak, Haida, and Athabascan—which is by far the largest.

At one time, Nadene peoples occupied much of Alaska and wide expanses of northwestern Canada; eventually, they reached into northern Mexico. Some of them were skilled fishermen, others were great hunters, and all were food gatherers who followed their preferred game and favored foodstuffs along various routes. Today, small enclaves still remain along the Pacific coast as far south as California; of these latter, the Tolawa and Hupa are representatives. What caused certain groups to come into the Southwest, and why they selected the routes they traveled, have been matters of conjecture in large part. However they came, they considered themselves to be "The People," the *Dine'é.*

A form of chronological evidence known as the lexicostatistic dating method, or glottochronology, places the divergences of these Dine'é from the northern Athabascan groups some seven hundred to a thousand years ago. Computations fix the southern movements at a time about one thousand years past, and continuing for approximately four hundred years (which fits well with traditions). This method, then, indicates that the arrival of Athabascans in the Southwest took place in the mid-fourteenth century, (*See* Hoijer 1956; Young, 1968:4) or slightly later.

Certain indications suggest that some of the Dine'é traveled through the intermontane region west of the Rocky Mountains (Willey 1966:232; Huscher 1942, 1943; Harrington 1940:523, 525, 527-529), but no evidence of this has been established. And archaeological findings of the last few years and historical references to a limited degree reveal that significant movements of Athabascans followed down the eastern slopes of the Rocky Mountains during the 1400's. Some of these migrants reached the southern limit of present day Colorado around 1500. Part of them edged eastward into southwestern Kansas, the panhandle of Oklahoma, and central-west Texas to become known as Kiowa-Apache. Certain of the bands continued southward, some centering in southwestern Texas as the Lipan Apache, others turned westward to occupy chosen locations in southwestern New Mexico and eastern Arizona. And those who were to become known as the Jicarilla Apache and the Navaho found their way westward through mountain passes which brought them into north-central New Mexico, into the upper reaches of the San Juan River.

The New Homeland The region into which the Jicarilla Apache and the Navaho found their way had been occupied by small numbers of village-dwelling peoples from about A.D. 400-700; after 700 until 1050, the population had increased. These facts are recognizable by distinct phases of Pueblo occupation. (*See* Eddy 1966) The district, then, like most of the Southwest, suffered long periods of drought during the late thirteenth century. It was not the first time this had happened. The significant fact which caused abandonment of pueblos and movements of people into more favorable areas was the shift from a summer dominent precipitation pattern to a winter pattern. Having occupied higher elevations where rainfall was sufficient for cultivation of crops, the change in precipitation with its shorter growing season caught the people living above what was an area of a sufficient growing season. They had either to revert to a Desert Culture economy—which meant the break up of large social units—or move. They moved. (*See* Schoenwetter and Dittert 1968; Eddy 1974) The Athabascans, because of their basic hunting and gathering economy, were able to exist in small groups. It is possible that the earliest of them coming into the Colorado-New Mexico border locations from the east were wandering raiders who, discovering the abandoned pueblos and adjoining lands of the upper San Juan, deemed it expedient to move into the then promising region. Several investigators of Navaho history have determined that the earliest area of Navaho occupation in the Southwest is the traditional *Dinetah*, meaning "among-the-people" in the Navaho language; this is identifiable as an area centering in the Gobernador and Largo tributaries of the San Juan river, about seventy-five miles northwest of Santa Fe.

CULTURAL CHARACTERISTICS

Through the preceding narration, it has become evident that the culture of the Pueblo Indians may receive additions which are grafted onto the basic social structure, and that losses may occur during time and from outside pressures or other contingencies; but change with regard to traditional mores, or lifeways, has been resisted resolutely. In the latter respect—change—adherence to a dual ceremonial organization dictated inflexibility; the Pueblos have held on with age-old tenacity. Major concern has been for an entire village or community, the *group as a whole*, with little thought for the individual, although changes in minor traits could take place.

In contrast, the Athapascan-speaking peoples have a culture system of completely opposite nature. With those of our special concern, the Navaho and his closely related cousins, the Apaches, who constitute a single ethnic group, sharing a common culture core, (Steward 1955:37) it is the *individual* who is of primary importance.

HABITAT AND SOCIAL ORGANIZATION

Fundamentally, each Athabascan band had its headman who selected a location for his people in an unoccupied district that provided good hunting and gathering opportunities. In the Southwest, they chose protected canyons and high plateaus, or mesas, with extensive grasslands and the timbered mountain fastnesses where game was plentiful. Constant streams were not so vital to these transient ones as they were to the sedentary peoples who dwelt in pueblos or other permanent communities. The Apaches and Navaho moved about at first, camping or living temporarily near good springs for the most part, or by small streams, ponds, or lakes. Residential shifting was seasonal in accordance with the climatic fluctuations that controlled food supply and forage.

From various lines of evidence, it is apparent that these newcomers followed a patrilineal system of descent, with patrilocal residence, and it is believed that they had "a shamanistic-individual religion preoccupied with curing," without priestly officers such as obtain among the Pueblo Indians (*See* Hester 1962:87) and without permanent religious structures.

As they passed along the eastern side of the Rocky Mountains, marginal to the great plains, the immigrants came into contact with Plains Indians (the Kiowa and others) who had culture traits unknown to the Athabascans. Being quick to see the advantages some of these features offered, they were promptly added to the meager trait list of the immigrants, who brought only the knowledge they could carry in their heads and things they could carry on their backs and perhaps the backs of dogs.

Among the possible additions to their original culture may have been conical dwellings of forked-stick construction or crude rock shelters and cylindrical pottery with roundly pointed bottoms—a Woodland type. The immigrants could have become familiar with agriculture from the Plains peoples. (*See* Willey 1966: 232) These items and knowledge, apparently, the Dine'é brought into the Southwest, with a new type of weapon, the sinew-backed bow which was a far more formidable instrument than the simple wooden bow long used by the Pueblos.

ORIGINS OF BAND NAMES

Accounts of the Spaniards, who entered the Southwest not long after the arrival of the Athabascans, make little reference to people who may have been of that subfamily. Chroniclers of the expedition of Coronado (1540-1542) made slight mention of

Indians who can be so identified; but the Espejo expedition of 1582 encountered a band near San Mateo (Mount Taylor), New Mexico, which was probably ancestral to the Cañoncito Navaho of present times. (Brugge 1969)

It is believed that the term "Apache" was derived from the Zuñi word, *ápachu*, meaning "enemy." The Spaniards appear to have met members of the southern bands first. To differentiate one group from another, they noted particular characteristics or locations. Those who gathered an agave species, *mescal*, for food were called "Apache de Mescalero," the Mescalero Apache. The ones that occupied the Chiricahua mountain strongholds became the Chiricahua Apache; and those farther north were designated as "Querechos," and later as the Gila, San Carlos, White Mountain, Tonto, Cibecue, and so on, utilizing regional terms. Because some of those who took up locations in the north made fine basketry containers which served purposes of small gourds, or *jicarillas*, with which the Spaniards were familiar, they were called "Apache de Jicarilla." And others who were found cultivating crops became "Apache de Návaju." This term is believed to have derived from the Tewa word *Návahu'u*, or "the arroyo with the cultivated fields."

FIRST SNOWFALL (Navaho)

The snow has come at last;
Coming down in soft flakes,
Caressing my face with tenderness
As if it were telling me,
"You are the first I've touched."
And, as I walk along,
The snowflakes seem to sing
A song that has never been heard,
A song that has never been sung—
Unheard!
Unsung!
Except in my heart.

By Tommy Smith

Winner of the Second Prize, Scottsdale National Indian Arts Exhibition, 1964.

From: *The Writers' Reader,* 1962-1966. Institute of American Indian Arts, Santa Fe, N. M.

.... THE NAVAHO INDIANS

According to their legends, the Navaho came to this earth through a progression of underworlds. The number of worlds may vary. In some versions these are recognized as numbering twelve, which are grouped by fours into three layers, or "rooms," known as the Black World, the Red World, and the Blue world, respectively. (*See* Young 1968: 2; Yazzie 1971) Again, four underworlds are recognized, the world in which we dwell, the sky immediately above, and one still higher—Land-beyond-the-sky. (*See* Reichard 1963: 14ff.)

It is believed that not only did The People originate in underworlds, but so did the land itself and all forms of water, the animals, all vegetation and other features. All were brought to the surface by supernatural beings. The place of emergence, *Xajiinai*, is considered to be a hole in La Plata Mountains of southwestern Colorado. The Navaho origin myth is long and detailed. (*See* Matthews 1897: 63–159; Schevill 1947: 29-48; Moon 1970)

Once in this region—tradition sets the time six hundred to eight hundred years ago—The People wandered about. As they say, "many groups joined the original people, to become the progenitors of the earliest clans." By accretion the groups grew, some coming "from the ancient pueblos; some from people who spoke a language similar to Navaho . . . ; and, at a later date, Mexicans and Utes." (Young 1968:2)

BRIEF HISTORY

The Beginnings of Change

Archaeologically, two phases of culture appear to be distinguishable in the Dinetah domain. The earlier one—as yet not clearly defined, due to a paucity of datable remains—brought the immigrants into contact with eastern Pueblo peoples. One of the results was that the Navaho, the interjacent ones, recognizing the Pueblo culture to be more advanced than their own, began to adopt practices which were advantageous to them. Modifying their hunting-gathering mode of life, they acquired horticultural knowledge and began raising corn, or maize. In time, farming brought about a semisedentary residence pattern.

Prior to the coming of the Spaniards, Pueblo peoples occupied river valleys from Old Mexico to northern New Mexico. Don Juan de Oñate brought the first Spanish colonists to settle in northern New Mexico in 1598, after which time comments were made about

Apache or Apachean peoples. Certain historical documents speak of them as raiders who, following attacks, were traced back by the Spaniards to their homes, where they were found to be growing corn—which suggests that these were Navaho.

Fray Zárata Salmerón first referred to the Navaho as a specific Apachean group, in 1626. By the third decade of the seventeenth century, the Navaho had became a large and powerful people, spreading from the Chama to the Little Colorado River, in eastern Arizona. Various bands had their recognized headmen; and it would seem that war and peace chiefs were distinguished. The Benavides report of 1630 refers to Apache and Navaho chiefs, as well as those of the Pueblos, without giving their names—as was common in the Spanish accounts.

The People were dwelling in earth-covered houses and were growing crops: corn, beans, squash, and other Southwestern products. They also gathered wild foods and hunted widely. And they engaged in extensive trade with other Indians and the Spanish settlers. They were holding large gatherings where dances were performed.

As the Spaniards increased in numbers, they edged into the desirable Pueblo holdings and demanded more and more of the Indians. Frequently, they attacked the pueblos, capturing or killing the people, or burning their structures. Prisoners were impressed into servitude or were sold as far south as Mexico. Undoubtedly, the Pueblos, resentful of the growing Spanish pressures and domination, encouraged attacks on them by the Apache-Navaho. At any rate, strife mounted and reprisals increased. Fray Alonso de Benavides, in 1630, published an account of conditions of the period. (*See* Young 1968:12-16; Forrestal 1954:44-52) He established contact with the Navaho and endeavored to achieve peace between the divers peoples and to introduce Christianity to the Indians—both without much success.

It was recorded that in 1653 a Spanish punitive expedition surprised some Navaho holding a native ceremonial. Although no pictographs or petroglyphs on the cliff walls or in caverns have been identified for the earlier archaeological period, it is possible that impermanent art portrayals (drypaintings?) may have been made in connection with ceremonials. The Spanish phraseology also suggests that, by the mid-seventeenth century, the Spaniards had asserted themselves to such a degree as to cause the Navaho, as well as the Pueblo Indians, to go underground, as it were, with their ceremonial practices.

After the Pueblo Revolt of 1680 and the reconquest of 1692, many of the pueblos were abandoned, and the Indians therefrom were pushed northward toward the San Juan, which brought them into significant contact with the Navaho. In some areas, the two peoples mingled. As a consequence, "In the space of a few years the Navaho adopted the Puebloan styles of architecture, manufacturing techniques, and religious paraphernalia, plus many elements of non-material culture such as clans, matrilineal descent, matrilocal residence, the origin myth, and ritual." (Hester 1962:91) But with these changes, the preferred residence of the Navaho continued to be the *hogan*, a house type traceable to the Asian World.

Immediately after 1696, sites of the upper San Juan consisted of open clusters of hogans and masonry *pueblitos*, or small pueblos, of three or four rooms, indicating that Pueblo refugees were living as isolated family units. Like settlements did not appear in the Gobernador and Largo canyons until some twenty years later, showing that the Navaho and the Pueblo refugees were moving southward.

Huge masonry compounds and pueblitos were built in the Gobernador, in defensive locations on high rock pinnacles. Some of the buildings were in the form of towers equipped with loopholes. Certain sites contained as many as forty rooms. It has been noted that the "only peculiarly Navaho architectural features were the hogans and sweat lodges inside the masonry compounds." (Schaafsma 1966:4)

Archaeologists have called the period dating from 1696 to 1775, the *Gobernador phase*. By the terminal date, Ute, Comanche and Spanish enemies had brought such pressure to bear on the Navaho that they had completely abandoned the eastern Dinetah— the area east of Blanco Canyon. For the Gobernador, data are much more numerous than for the pre-1696 phase. The economic pattern included hunting and gathering of wild plants, with some herding and dry farming. Water was controlled by storage behind sand dikes in a few instances. By 1706, herds of sheep, goats, horses, and cattle were kept—all Spanish introductions. Corrals and horsegear have been found in archaeological excavations. And pecked and painted depictions of people are portrayed on the cliffs—some as black-robed friars on horseback, some wearing fringed attire of Plains Indians, and others with manta-like garments of the Pueblos; with these are *yé'ii* figures (Holy People), eagles, corn plants, bison, and a variety of symbols.

During the earliest part of the eighteenth century, the Pueblo culture dominated the San Juan basin; the Navaho had adopted it in full force. However, in the last half of the century, Pueblo traits were modified or simplified; and by the end of the period, with abandonment of the upper San Juan-Gobernador-Largo districts, the refugees had been absorbed by the Navaho. (*See* Schaafsma 1966:9)

Pueblo and Navaho ceremonial paraphernalia have been excavated from the same caches, giving credence to the belief that much modern Navaho ceremonialism is derived from early Pueblo contacts. Pueblo influences—including sandpaintings, metate and firepit styles, and weaving at least in part—altered the basic Navaho culture, and within a few centuries, distinguished it from that of the Apaches who were less in contact with the Pueblo peoples.

Not the least of the changes was in the spoken language. At the time of the entrada of Coronado, the Athabascan groups spoke closely related, if not essentially similar tongues. Linguists have calculated that the Navaho and Chiricahua Apache were close relatives and historically very friendly, and that their languages became distinctive one from the other during a period of only 149 years. (Hoijer 1963; but *see* Schroeder 1963:17) The Navaho, by the same calculation, are separated by 279 years from the San Carlos and Jicarilla Apaches, and by 335 years from the Lipan Apache. (*See* Young 1968:4)

Shifts of Location   The folklore of the Navaho, as well as their symbolic portrayals on available rock surfaces, and archaeological remains traces their movements from the original locations in the upper San Juan region, down through the Gobernador, Largo and Blanco, into Chaco Canyon and to the Big Band Mesa districts some thirty or forty years later; there, Navaho ceremonial art appears to be relatively scarce. Farther to the west, where Canyon de Chelly in northeastern Arizona was settled by Navaho people before the earlier sites in New Mexico were abandoned, some of the initial art forms seem to have proliferated, while others are absent. Tree-ring dates for archaeological remains have been found to show later occupation going from east to west.

In one instance, however, investigations at an archaeological site at the base of Mariana Mesa, some ten miles north of Quemado in west-central New Mexico, are said to have yielded "the earliest tree-ring date yet obtained from a Navajo forked-pole hogan—

1387." Fifteen additional tree-ring dates supporting the antiquity of this site were also obtained. (Navajo Tribal Museum 1968*) Perhaps this late fourteenth century dwelling was inhabited by migrant Athabascan people who entered the Southwest by an intermontane route, rather than by the common trails leading into north-central New Mexico.

In general, each Navaho community had certain individuals known as men of wealth, with influence, ceremonial knowledge, and good judgment. These usually were referred to as *naat'áani*, or headmen (men—peace leaders—who always knew the Blessingway, which is intended to gain the good will of Navaho supernaturals and to bring good fortune; it is not primarily curative). (*See* Van Valkenburgh 1945:71-72; Shepardson 1963:78)

The White Intruders Numerous accounts have been written of the Navaho and Apache during the years following their entrance into the Southwest and the decades that saw them fighting against many odds, including other Indian peoples and, especially, the white men who came in ever-increasing numbers—the Spaniards and then the Anglo-Americans. References to pertinent publications are given in the bibliography of this book.

Juan Bautista de Anza, who served as governor of New Mexico from 1778-1789, initiated a plan whereby Navaho headmen were called "captains" or "generals" in the Spanish army. At that time, a prominent Navaho known as Antonio el Pinto was recognized as a general. He received gifts regularly from the Spaniards and was influential in maintaining peaceful conditions until the time of his death in 1793. This type of bribery was carried on after Mexican rule prevailed.

Early years of the nineteenth century were filled with strife, with short periods of peace. The first treaty that defined a boundary between the Spaniards and the Navaho was agreed upon in 1819. The population center was then in Canyon de Chelly, from which westward movements were made into the canyon and valley lands of Chinle, Black Mesa, Navajo Mountain, Klagetoh, and Steamboat Canyon.

Mexican control covered the period from 1821 to 1846. From the time of the arrival of General S. W. Kearny with the U. S. Army, in the latter year, the Americans made intermittent attempts to achieve peace with the Navaho, who were warring and

*This interpretation is questioned by other archaeologists.

raiding. Through the mid-nineteenth century, a few Navaho chiefs were identified by name. Antonio Sandoval was mentioned as leader of the Cebolleta Navaho band. He was a "medicine man." The renowned chief, man of great wisdom and foresight, Narbona, comes to attention, and Zarcillos Largos. When a treaty was signed by Colonel A. W. Doniphan and the Navaho on 22 November 1846, these three were signers (with "X" marks), as were: Caballada Mucha, Alexandro, Kiatanito, José Largo, Segundo, Pedro José, Manuelito, Tapia, Archulette, and Juanico and Savoiette García. (Young 1968:33-34) Much has been written of these chiefs and other historical figures.

Treaties were proposed, some made (always with communication difficulties) and shortly broken. By 1849, American emigrants were crossing the Southwest in their rush for gold in California. It was common practice for them to abuse and take advantage of the Indians—Navaho, Pueblos, and others alike. Increasing encroachment of the Anglo-Americans on lands which the Navaho considered to be their own, added to misunderstandings and mounting violence. It is recorded that by 1858 the Navaho lived "scattered over a wide area, from the Jémez Mountains to the Hopi Country and from the San Juan River to the region south of the Little Colorado." (Young 1968:38; *see* Harrington 1945:514, fig. 32)

Forts and garrisons established by the U.S. to control Navaho uprisings were left unmanned, in general, following the outbreak of the Civil War of 1861. The Navaho and Apaches were quick to take advantage of the situation and soon were the scourge of the countryside. A few army troops did engage in war against them rather ineffectually. Then it was that Colonel Christopher (Kit) Carson, of Taos, was called to lead a campaign that was destined to bring the turmoil to an end. On 20 July 1863, he and his troops, joined by a band of Ute Indians, reached Fort Defiance, Arizona, to fulfill the ruthless policy formulated by General James Carleton who, in the first place, proposed to resettle the Navaho and Apaches. On a reservation created at Fort Sumner, New Mexico, they were to become farmers like the Pueblos. All captives who surrendered voluntarily would be taken there and all male Navaho who resisted were to be shot. Their livestock and food supplies were to be destroyed; and they were.

Days of Captivity   As under Spanish oppression, the Navaho scattered into isolated canyons, attempting to avoid Carleton's attacks. From November, 1863, nevertheless, captives were rounded up and forced to go to

Fort Sumner, or *Bosque Redondo* . . . on the Long Walk. By December, 1864, the Navaho there numbered 8,354; and 405 Mescalero Apache were confined there also. The next year, it was reported that 6,447 Navaho were concentrated at Fort Sumner, and it was estimated that 1,200 had escaped captivity and remained in Navaholand. (*See* Young 1968:41) Chiefs Manuelito and Barboncito eluded Kit Carson's roundup and refused to surrender to the army. They and other chiefs held out in their isolated locations.

The Carleton experiment was a horrible failure. Crops that the Navaho and Apaches were forced to plant produced a disheartening yield; confinement, and crowded and unnatural conditions resulted in discontent and disease and great numbers of deaths. The enormity of Carleton's despotic regime was finally recognized and he was relieved of his command in the fall of 1866. The following January, custody of the Navaho was returned to the BIA.

On 1 June 1868, a treaty was concluded and on 12 August of that year, it was signed, establishing a 3.5 million acre reservation for the Navaho within their old domain. Signers of the document were W. T. Sherman and S. F. Tappan of the Indian Peace Commission, and twelve Navaho chiefs: Barboncito, Armijo, Delgado, Manuelito, Largo, Herrero, Chiquito, Muerto de Hombre (Biwos), Hombro, Narbona, Narbono Segundo, and Ganado Mucho. All signed with "X" marks. (*See* Link 1968)

Though this was but a small portion of their former holdings, the Navaho were jubilant. Many tribulations, however, had to be met and endured before the return to their homeland was actually accomplished. Old Fort Fauntleroy, renamed Fort Wingate, was reactivated in 1868 and served as an agency for the returning Navaho for a time. Then the agency was moved to Fort Defiance.

Political Reorganization: The Tribal Council

As late as 1922, no political body that could be considered as tribal existed among the Navaho. Chapters were initiated in 1927 on a community level, where two types of leaders were recognized: formal and informal. The informal leaders, in some communities at least, are influential men who to a certain extent continue the traditional naat'áani system. (*See* Young 1961:371ff.; Hill 1940) Showing something of the counterbalance, or dichotomy, of Navaho social organization is the fact that war leaders were recognized also—men who always knew the Warway.

Formal leaders came to hold elective offices in the chapters and/or agencies of broader authority. Chapter officers are a president, vice-president, and secretary.

The Navaho population was increasing significantly and the people's relations with the rest of the nation were growing more and more complex. Need for an entity that could serve the interests of all the Navaho people became critical. A Business Council, on which three influential Navaho served, was established. Its first meeting was held on 7 July 1923. One of the three was Henry Chee Dodge, who had served as Navaho interpreter for some years. Intelligent, educated, and with great leadership abilities, he "became the ladder along which the Navajo people tortuously made their way out of the early post-treaty period into the modern age." (Young 1968:50)   Chee Dodge was leader of the Navaho for over seventy years. Organization of the Business Council was only a step toward a workable arrangement. Gradual developments continued. Fifteen years later, a tribal council was formed; and this led to organization of the Navajo Tribal Council in 1938. By 1950, this was well established and "the tribe was fast becoming a political entity." (Young 1968:63)

After a Century   Now a century has passed and successive generations of Navaho have come into being since the days at Fort Sumner. Only a few of the old ones lived to witness the Centennial observances which were prominently featured during 1968. Varieties of activities were held, including a re-enactment of the Long Walk to Bosque Redondo; and a series of publications was issued. In these, one finds a wealth of information concerning the Navaho of the past and of today (*see* bibliography).

As one views modern maps, he may locate the Navaho domain generally as the region bounded on the northeast by the Continental Divide, on the southeast by the Río Puerco, on the south by the San José and Puerco rivers,* on the west by the Little Colorado and Colorado rivers, and on the north by the San Juan River. The entire area, broadly speaking, is an almost level plateau, averaging some 5,500 feet in elevation. In places, however, mountains rise to a height of more than 10,000 feet, and deep, sheer-walled canyons cut into the plateau. This results in spectacular landscape, with isolated mesas and buttes, desert wastes, arroyos that are usually dry channels—but which, in seconds, may become raging torrents

---

*In accord with a decision rendered by the United States Board of Geographical Names between 1 July 1936 and 30 June 1937, it should be understood that the Puerco River "rises in township 16N, range 13W, McKinley County, New Mexico, and flows west and southwest to join the Little Colorado in Navajo County, Arizona. Henceforth [the Board stated] this stream will be known as the *Puerco River* and not the Río Puerco or Río Puerco of the west." (Southwestern Monuments 1937)

that gouge out the earth and cause erosional destruction. The topography is matched by great contrasts in climate. Winters are cold and summers are hot; and, always, insufficient moisture renders the country marginal insofar as agricultural pursuits are concerned. Only the arroyos and limited areas on which water can be utilized by gravity flow are suitable for farming ... unless modern irrigation techniques are employed. And these are slow in coming to Navaholand. Steps have been taken by the BIA to train the Navaho in modern farming methods, and the tribe has appropriated hundreds of thousands of dollars for the training program.

THE MAIN NAVAHO RESERVATION

Land holdings of the Navaho have been increased periodically and substantially since the days of their return from Fort Sumner. But never have the increases kept abreast of the growing need of the people. The main reservation now embraces 14,450,369 acres, or about 25,000 square miles, reaching out from the Four Corners to include northeastern Arizona, northwestern New Mexico, and southwestern Utah, in that order of acreage. Much of the land is desert and semidesert, sandy or rocky and of little productive value. In some districts, 240 acres are necessary for pasturage for one sheep for a year. Approximately 68,000 acres are farmlands. The acreage under irrigation varies, including federally planned projects and others not formally designated. Perhaps 10,000 acres are now under irrigation. And the population is ever growing. Brandon (1969:14) says they are growing "twice as fast as the national average. The people want to stay together as members of living communities." The Navaho registered as of 1 January 1970 were 126,267. (Navaho Census Office, Window Rock, Arizona) Not all Navaho are registered, so the total number is several thousand more than this figure.

With the completion of a dam on the San Juan River and the diversion canals in prospect, 110,000 acres of irrigable land should be added. When water becomes available, however, it will not give the Navaho what they desire for the most part—land and water for individual working and production. Rather, large commercial enterprises are destined to control the water; and most of the Navaho will be laborers for "the other fellow." Some 36,000 acres are dry-farmed.

Until the present time, the Navaho never settled in communities that could be called villages or towns. They lived in desirable locations scattered over the entire reservation. Following the matrilineal pattern, a Navaho grandmother is the center of the family. The children belong to her and are members of her clan. Because it is taboo for a Navaho man to look at his mother-in-law, or to talk with her, a woman and her husband do not live with the wife's mother. Instead, they erect a home nearby, so that the woman and her children can frequent the maternal abode. Thus, one may find several generations dwelling together or in proximity: grandmother, mother, daughter, and grandchildren. It is usual for the dwelling, the crops, and the livestock to be cared for by the mother and her children, so these are owned by the woman.

Inasmuch as property ownership among the Navaho is individual, a woman disposes of the rugs she weaves, and of her crops and stock; she spends her money however she chooses. A man does likewise with his silver jewelry, with the wages he earns, and with the income from his stock raising or farming. It is the man who represents the family in public and at ceremonials.

Visit Navaholand   To see the Navaho properly, one must go into their own country—far afield, and often over dirt roads. Road construction and maintenance were long neglected on the vast, thinly populated expanses. Today, however, hundreds of miles of black-top highways have been, and are being, built on the main reservation, and even more of graveled roadways. Some Navaho may be found around the trading posts and stores, buying groceries, clothing and supplies, or pawning or selling their jewelry, radios, cameras, moccasins, rugs or blankets, belts, and miscellaneous items. Occasionally, one comes upon them by accident, herding their sheep or crowding the animals around a water hole or tank.

The typical Navaho dwelling, the hogan, is usually round or hexagonal, sometimes octagonal, constructed of logs and mud, or sometimes of rocks, with a central air vent in the ceiling. (*See* Richards 1970:8-9) Rarely are more than two or three together, and a traveler is likely to pass by without seeing them in daytime—so well do they blend with the natural setting; in the evening, one is surprised at the number of fires whose flickering light gives evidence of the Navaho dwelling or camp near at hand.

Near the hogan or under the shelter of a brush-covered ramada, Navaho women may be seen weaving rugs on an upright loom, which was adopted from the Pueblo Indians. Textile belts are woven on a loom made from a forked branch of a juniper tree. When in use, this is erected on a slight diagonal in front of the seated weaver. Small children will be playing nearby, or perhaps helping to card the wool. The older children and the husband are usually away, herding sheep or on an errand to the trading post. This picture is not so easily found today as the pattern of life is ever changing by acculturation. The Navaho rug is becoming a relatively scarce article.

Away from their homeland, Navaho Indians are seen at Pueblo ceremonies, especially at Jémez, Laguna, Zuñi, and in the Hopi villages. They come to trade and barter, to sell rugs and jewelry and to take home agricultural products and other Pueblo items. A few Navaho may be seen on the streets of Cuba, Santa Fe or Albuquerque. Their numbers increase as one goes westward; in Farmington, Gallup, Flagstaff, and other towns nearby they make up a considerable segment of the population. Part of the year, they are conspicuous in the southern Colorado towns where they go to work in the beet fields or engage in other work. In their "capital city," Window Rock, and places on the Navaho reservation, such as Shiprock, Chinle, Tuba City, Ganado, Fort Defiance, and Crown-point, they are naturally predominant. It may be noted that each of these communities has a hospital or health center, and also a boarding school.

PHYSICAL APPEARANCE AND ATTIRE The Navaho tend to be taller than the Pueblo Indians, and most of them are slender. They have long, somewhat raw-boned faces and a number of the men have mustaches. Back of the heads are flattened by cradleboards on which infants are carried. A typical Navaho woman might be described as having small arms, hands and feet, with thin legs; long face, nose and chin; and thick lips. The slanted, oriental eye is fairly common among women and children. Their particular style of walking and their manner of making gestures are identifying characteristics of Navaho people.

A few old Navaho men still may wear the attire of earlier days, at least in part. But in the main, clothing, like that of other Indian men, has come to be that of the western stereotype: blue denim pants worn with an ornamental belt, cowboy boots or heavy shoes; colorful shirts and kerchiefs, large felt or straw hats, or maybe a bright headband, coat or leather jacket. Particularly on special occasions, silver and turquois jewelry is worn. If the occasion demands, dress clothing, even tuxedos, may be worn.

The female attire has shown less change through the years. Until recently, most women and girls wore garments reflecting the style of the 1860's, when the Navaho women began to wear long, full skirts of calico or some other colorful material, and velveteen blouses—these from patterns that were supplied during the Fort Sumner days. A bright red woven belt and high-top laced shoes of tan leather would often complete the costume. Some years ago, bobby socks became popular and many Navaho women may be seen wearing them with saddle oxfords. Nevertheless, the traditional moccasins of deerskin and cowhide are still in evidence to some degree.

The Pendleton blanket, or one of similar manufacture or appearance, is a favorite of both men and women, worn about the shoulders or folded over an arm. These attractive, machine-made products often have been admired by newcomers to the Southwest as *Indian blankets*, which, indeed, they have become—by adoption only. (The Pendleton Woolen Mills of Portland, Oregon, long ago sent designers to the Southwest where they spent a great deal of time with the Navaho. They learned the symbolism and Navaho preferences. "Using this knowledge they then designed blankets in the Indian concept and in the colors and patternings the Indians most desired." (Eklund 1969) The Pueblos and other Indian peoples have distinct preferences also as to designs and colors.)

Entrance into a new era is observable as more and more Navaho people abandon their attractive clothing for the styles of their non-Indian neighbors. Professional dress designers have adapted the old style full-skirted garments and bedecked blouses of the Navaho women, and they market these gay frocks as "squaw dresses" or "fiesta dresses"; these have found favor among the young Navaho women and tourists alike.

The universal badge of distinction among the Navaho is the silver and turquois jewelry—rings, bracelets, necklaces, earrings, buttons and pins, hatbands, and even shoe buckles. But don't let this display of wealth deceive you. It may indicate something of the wearer's own prosperity, but most likely—especially if worn at a ceremonial or public gathering—it represents his borrowings from family and friends or from a nearby trading post operator. A Navaho frequently arranges to remove valuable belongings from pawn with a trader for display at special functions.

CONTEMPORARY LIFE

Herdsman vs. Farmer

Differences between the Navaho and the Pueblos are deeper than clothing, stature, or spoken tongue. The heritage of each is quite disparate. The Pueblo is a house-dweller and horticulturist, first and last; the Navaho is a herdsman basically and for that reason follows a shifting pattern of life. Kluckhohn has stressed the fact that the

Navaho has never been a nomad. (*See* Kluckhohn and Leighton 1962:38-39) Although the Navaho practice agriculture to some extent today, and engage in livestock raising, these sources of income are significantly augmented by miscellaneous revenues from other resources, such as timber (of which there are over 472,700 acres of commercial value), oil, gas, vanadium, uranium, coal, sand and gravel. The Navaho tribe is in big business, totaling in the millions, which requires employment of skilled attorneys, business men, and officials. Per capita personal income averaged around $772 in 1969.

Education   After decades during which the Navaho saw little reason to send their youngsters to the white man's schools, or to schools following ordinary white man's curriculums, their attitude has altered. Now, instead of resisting the federal efforts to live up to education stipulations made in the treaty of 1868, the Navaho have come to realize that the young should be trained to cope with modern demands. (*See* Smith, A. M. 1965, 1966, 1968) Consequently, the tribe and individuals as well exert their influence toward having adequate schooling for the young; and also they promote adult education.

Children from beginners through high school are enrolled in reservation schools. As they progress, they are taught skills and trades. Some of the schools are located in isolated regions, away from all other structures. Most of the pupils in these remote schools are picked up by bus and travel distances as much as fifteen miles, or more; and they may have to walk a mile or more from home to the bus stop. The majority of the children entering these schools are unable to speak other than their native tongue, Navaho. The BIA operates a five-year program in general education in several off-reservation schools. The Navaho Tribe has set up a multi-million dollar trust fund for scholarships for qualified Navaho high school graduates to attend colleges or universities of their choice. More than 46,000 young Navaho people now attend school regularly. (Anonymous 1972)

A community college was opened in January, 1969, in borrowed quarters at Many Farms, Arizona, a community of some 2,000 population. This is the only college established on an Indian reservation or to be sponsored by Indian people. Its success and growth resulted in the planning of a beautiful campus for the Navajo Community College in the Ponderosa pine forests north of Fort Defiance, near Tsaile Lake, on 1,200 acres of land provided by the tribal council. (Navaho Community College 1969) Loans totaling $2,530,000 were approved by U.S. Department of Housing and Urban Development for use in constructing the college; and a number of significant grants have been made by foundations and commercial organizations for its operation. The new site of the college was dedicated on 13 April 1971, with some two thousand people attending the ceremonies. The plans are conceived to reflect Navaho culture in design and construction. Target date for the completion of the first phase of construction and occupancy was set for April, 1972.

The college, whose president is a Navaho, early achieved correspondent accreditation status from the North Central Association of Colleges and Secondary Schools, and started working for full accreditation. Its program revolves around an Indian studies program, with the study work geared to the individual who does not have a great deal of education. It teaches what the Indian wants to learn—Navaho history, arts and crafts, and, among other things, driver's training. Any Navaho over eighteen years of age who applies for entrance is accepted. Of the spring enrollment for 1971, eighty per cent of the 571 enrolled strudents were Navaho; 10 per cent were Indians of other groups; and 10 per cent were non-Indian. About one-third of the thirty-five-member faculty are Navaho. On 4 May 1971, seventeen students were graduated from the college.

Modern Government   To this day, the Navaho continue their organization based on regulations promulgated by the Secretary of Interior. Modifications are made as occasion demands "by the governing body itself, with the consent and approval of the Secretary, rather than an institution based on a constitutional framework approved by the people it represents." (Young 1968:61) The governing body is composed of a chairman, vice-chairman, and seventy-four delegates elected on a land management district basis. Elections are held every four years; campaigning becomes active at these times. Voters, both men and women over twenty-one years of age, must register; voting is done by secret ballot. Women can and do serve on the tribal council. The term is four years. All officers are sworn in by a District Judge from Arizona or New Mexico.

Council meetings are held in the Council House at Window Rock, a structure built in octagonal shape like a huge hogan. Each member of the council has a desk with his or her name on it. Meetings are conducted entirely by the Navaho; Indian Service personnel are available for consultation but do not participate unless requested. A number of committees serve, such as the Advisory Committee (which is comparable to the Cabinet of the federal government), and smaller bodies, each attending to specific duties. A trained and uniformed Navaho police force is selected by the Advisory Committee. Surrounding the council chamber is a complex of administration buildings in which offices and necessary facilities are housed.

In 1969, the Advisory Committee, serving as the executive arm of the Tribal Council, directed the council "and all departments, divisions, agencies, enterprises, and entities of the Navajo Tribe to use the phrase 'Navajo Nation' in describing the lands and people of the Navajo Tribe." Furthermore, the Advisory Committee directed that "all resolutions of the Tribal Government be certified as being duly enacted at Window Rock, Navajo Nation (Arizona)." Perhaps in way of explanation, it was stated: "The Treaty of 1868 recognized the Navajo People as a sovereign nation and spelled 'Navajo' with a 'j'." This, incidentally, is in direct contrast with the feeling of the Navaho council members of a few years ago. At the council meetings then held, the federal government was entreated to spell the tribal designation with an "h," the Navaho saying that they were among the "first Americans," and that they preferred the Americanized spelling. The government took no heed of their pleas. Scholars agree with the older Navaho sentiment. (*See* Trager 1969)

A tribal Parks Commission was created in 1957, and it has recently become very active. One of its important duties is to protect the hundreds of prehistoric ruins that are located within the confines of the Navaho reservation. These are considered to be among the tribe's irreplaceable assets, and great efforts are made to protect them from vandalism and "pot hunting." A reward of one hundred dollars ($100) has been posted for information that will lead to the arrest and conviction of anyone illegally excavating in the ruins. Violators can be fined up to five hundred dollars ($500) or not more than ninety days in prison, or both.

Parks and visitor centers have been developed, guided tours have been organized, tourist accommodations developed over the vast reservation, and arts and crafts promoted. Annual fairs are held, as well as the many scheduled and unscheduled ceremonials, sings, rodeos, rug auctions, and other events. For information, visitors to Navaholand are directed to write to the Navajo Parks and Recreation Department, P. O. Box 418, Window Rock, Arizona, 86515.

Industrial and commercial developments on the reservation have had increasing impact on the Navaho people. A number of years ago, the Navajo Arts and Crafts Guild was initiated to encourage production of reservation items and to serve as a commercial outlet therefor. This is now located at Window Rock; it supplies Navaho arts and crafts productions to centers located at other vantage points on the reservation and elsewhere.

Electric power lines have been strung across the reservation and underground pipe lines for oil and gas and water crisscross the terrain. These have made possible large industrial undertakings. In 1960, the Navaho established the Navajo Tribal Utility Authority (NTUA) with headquarters at Fort Defiance to supply electricity, gas, sewerage, and water to the people and installations on the reservation. It is a multimillion dollar operation, employing some one hundred and eighty technically skilled Navaho.

The vast timberlands have been utilized, from simple sawmill operations to a sophisticated lumbering industry. First was a lumber camp at Sawmill, Arizona, which came to produce around twenty million board feet of lumber annually. Then, the tribal council appropriated eleven million dollars for new sawmill operations in the Chuska Mountains along the Arizona-New Mexico border. There, a whole new town, Navajo, New Mexico, has been established about twenty miles north of Window Rock. The plans are to cut approximately fifty million board feet a year for a decade, and then level off at about thirty-eight million board feet annually on a sustained yield basis.

Wisely, the Navaho elected five long-time western lumbermen to its board of directors and hired an expert manager for the new sawmill. The employment schedule there is about 325 Navaho; while some 150 work at the old mill. The Navajo Forest Products Industries now produces lumber and wood products for nationwide distribution.

In the mid-1950's, forward-looking companies concerned with the development of fuel components and power began to prospect in promising locations on the Navaho reservation. El Paso Natural Gas Company of El Paso, Texas, leased nearly 100,000 acres in the Burnham area, some fifty miles south of Farmington, New Mexico, with a view to possible strip-mining operations. Explorations revealed a potential of 519 million tons of strippable coal in the whole area.

The Utah Construction & Mining Company (now Utah

International, Inc.), headquartered in San Francisco, leased a twenty-five mile long strip of Navaho coal land and got a 50,000 acre-foot water allotment on the San Juan River from the New Mexico State Engineer. Currently, at Fruitland, New Mexico, huge draglines, one of which weighs four million pounds, strip away dirt and rock to a depth of as much as 120 feet to expose a low grade coal seam. This is then blasted for shoveling and hauling of the coal to the Fruitland power plant. In 1970, this mine was expected to produce around 8.5 million tons of coal per year—more than any other mine in the world at that time. At an agreed rate of fifteen cents a ton, the revenue—royalty and lease rentals—to the Navaho tribe was estimated at $1.3 million. (*See* Montgomery 1970b; 1970d)

The Navaho employed in the mine and generating plant benefit economically from this industrial undertaking, and from several similar or related projects. But the tremendous amounts of water required for cooling the generating plants arouse deep concern of far-seeing conservationists who realize that the mining of water may have detrimental results of increasing significance. Also, smoke and millions of tons of fly ash and chemicals fill the air and are deposited annually over a wide area.

A related multimillion dollar coal mining project under lease involves the Navaho and Hopi Indians, covering Black Mesa (the Navaho "female mountain") south of Kayenta and extending southwestward to the Hopi villages. There, the Peabody Coal Company of St. Louis, Missouri, arranged to operate on a 60,000 acre area where it is estimated that some 16 billion tons of coal occur at two main levels. Some 350 to 400 million tons of coal appear to be economically feasible for strip mining. The project is to furnish fuel for power generating plants at Mohave Station in southern Nevada and at Page, Arizona, on the Navaho reservation. Page originated in the 1950's as the construction camp for the building of the Glen Canyon Dam. The generating plant there is now under construction.

Huge draglines remove the ground cover of grass and piñon trees, and great shovels lift the thirty to forty feet of overburden and gouge out giant bites of coal. Water is being mined from sources built up during millions of years, from a depth of 2,000 feet or more below the top of Black Mesa. The water pours into a pipe of eighteen-inch diameter and is mixed with an equal part of finely pulverized coal for transportation along a 273-mile slurry line to the Mohave plant—thus being expected to move 117 million tons of coal over a period of thirty-five years. This pumping of water is calculated by certain water experts to result in the lowering of the watertable around Kayenta by one hundred feet. Water required for the thirty-five years' pumping is calculated to be 33,000 acre feet a year. It is purchased from the Navaho tribe at $7.50 per acre foot. An eighty-mile electric railroad, costing $40 million, is designed to deliver the coal from Black Mesa to the plant at Page. Water is to be derived from Lake Powell. (Montgomery 1970d)

Peabody's 1967 contract "called for a rental annually of $1 an acre the first five years of the lease and $2 an acre thereafter for the life of the lease on the 60,000 acre plot of mesaland." (Montgomery 1970c:A5)

All aspects of these monumental undertakings are envisioned as resulting in millions of dollars of income for the outside companies and subsidiaries, sizeable salaries for a small number of Indians and lesser sums for others. It has been estimated that in the period 1963-1970, some $4 million in tribal funds were expended in efforts to bring new industries to the reservation. BIA statistics for 1969 and 1970 show the Navaho labor force to be slightly over 38,000, and of these, nearly 45 percent were said to be out of work. New industries are credited with having produced 2,300 new jobs in the past five years. (Anonymous 1969b)

It is inevitable that the landscape of Navaholand will be altered, although present contracts call for restoration of the land to some degree. The natural beauty will be changed forever, as will be the centuries-old lifeways of the aboriginal inhabitants of the region.

Other undertakings are not so overwhelming or disturbing. General Dynamics Corporation has a plant at Fort Defiance. At Page, by the Glen Canyon Dam, is a Vostrom Electronics installation. (But occupation by dissident Indians led to Fairchild Semiconductor Division's closing its Shiprock plant in 1975, putting many Navaho out of work.)

Early in 1969, a supermarket chain, FedMart Corporation, opened a large shopping center in Window Rock, with low cost prices—an innovation on the reservation. Other commercial ventures are starting where industrial areas are growing—Colonel Sander's Kentucky Fried Chicken, for instance, and banks and service enterprises. And with expansion of businesses, new housing projects are keeping pace. Some homes are privately financed. Over six hundred Low Rent Housing units have been erected under the Navajo Housing Authority; and Mutual Help units are being built with families achieving equity through participation in the construction. More than 2,000 Navaho have taken part in a home improvement program, adding needed space, a new roof, or completing sanitary facilities.

The Navaho have appointed a Planning Board to work toward a total program of land use, participation of local people in determining their role in the community development, to meet the needs of child care, delinquency, education, care of the ill and elderly, and in making their homeland better for future generations.

During April, 1971, the community of Piñon scored a first on the reservation with the opening and blessing of a retail cooperative called the DINE-BI-NAA-YEI Cooperative. It is a dues-paying member of the Arizona Grocers Association. Open six days a week in the remodeled old arts and crafts building of the Piñon chapter house, it is operated solely by and primarily for the Navaho people of Piñon, which is located on reservation Route 4, between Second Mesa and Chinle. Members pay a one-dollar fee. Expectations were that the enterprise would be grossing about one thousand dollars a day. Federal funds, those of the Navaho, and of others were utilized in this undertaking.

In June of 1971, the Navaho took a historic step toward more independence from the federal government with the signing of an agreement to take over the federal commodity food program on their reservation.

Many of the younger Navaho and government officials want innovations to come to the reservation, and their views are coming to prevail in tribal elections. Jobs, changes in traditional concepts, and urbanization become increasingly important factors. A BIA official has said "if the economy can be stepped up, we can see sizeable towns develop." And he remarked that the Navaho are "very rapidly urbanizing and modernizing." (Graves 1970:24 August) One of the Navaho men deeply interested in the welfare of his people has pointed out the need for services on the reservation and, like others, he realizes the ever-growing need for more water.

At the same time, economic growth on the reservation is viewed with concern by the "traditional" Navaho who want to continue living as they have in the past. The opposing points of view result in conflicts. This is not a new trait in Navaho culture, but certain conflicts result in mental illnesses which old practices no longer control. Although youthful suicides are all but unheard of among many Indian groups, such as the Pueblos, the Navaho now have an exceptionally high rate of suicide. (*See* Levy 1965; Levy et al. 1969:124-147) Speaking of this, Dr. Karl Menninger says: "Where one commits suicide, scores are in despair."

The poem at the end of this chapter, on page 142, gives a Navaho's arresting commentary on white man's progress vs. Indian tradition.

Off-Reservation Employment
An increasing number of Navaho take off-reservation employment each year. This may be seasonal, with a Navaho working for a few months and then returning home to spend the remaining months with his family; with the development of industries on or near the reservation, jobs become longer lasting. In addition, an ever-growing number are leaving the reservation and settling in industrial areas. For these, employment is relatively permanent. Many thousands now live in Los Angeles, San Francisco, Oakland, Denver, Chicago, Dallas, and other cities. Such resettlement has been successful only when the Navaho has had sufficient education, hand skills, and understanding of non-Indian culture.

During times of war or other national stresses, the Navaho—both men and women—have made fine records in the armed forces, and in supporting industries. Today, they are well represented in most branches of the armed services.

HOPI-NAVAHO LAND DISPUTES
Through the years, Navaho and Hopi dissatisfaction over the lands supposedly shared between them has increased. Each became more and more vocal about the matter, and press notices on the subject appeared frequently. During early 1970, the news media carried extensive accounts of Navaho claims and Hopi briefs that had been presented to the federal Indian Claims Commission (a body established by Congress in 1946 to adjudicate and settle, once and for all, Indian claims against the U.S.A. "for unconscionable acts in previous years that had injured or unjustly deprived Indian tribes of lands and resources.") (*See* Young 1968:75) After hearing pro and con arguments, the commission finally laid down boundary lines involving about thirty million acres, and ruled that the Navaho should have been compensated therefor in the 1868 treaty. The Navaho will not get the land—whatever the specific acreage is computed to be—but they are entitled to a cash settlement from the government. It is intended that much of the money the Navaho are to receive will be used for industrial development of the tribe.

With this much accomplished, the Navaho set out to have legislation introduced which would add 240,000 acres to their reservation. They are seeking land adjoining the southeast corner of the Navaho reservation and jutting out toward Gallup and Zuñi. The bulk of the acreage is U.S. public domain held by the Bureau of Land Management, with a small amount of state land. Later, they look toward the checkerboard area, where they want to have several hundred thousand acres transferred to their reservation. It is a fact that Navaho have for some time been buying privately owned ranches east of the reservation. This has enabled them to get grazing permits on the adjacent public domain.

NAVAHO CEREMONIES

Among the Pueblo peoples, weather control—placing great emphasis on rainmaking—is fundamental in religious organization and ceremonial enactments under the control of priests. In contrast, Navaho religion centers in curing ceremonies directed by shamans following a system of imitative and sympathetic magic. All Navaho rituals are performed with certain aims in mind: restoring health, securing food, insuring survival. In the Navaho universe, two classes of personal forces are recognized, human beings and the Holy People, or supernatural beings—holy in that they are powerful and mysterious. The Navaho believes his universe functions according to certain set rules. If one learns these rules and lives in accordance with them, he will keep safe or be restored to safety. The Holy People have great powers over the people on earth; on the other hand, they may not only be supplicated and propitiated, but may be coerced as well.

The Navaho greatly fears death and everything connected with it. This intense feeling—a trait traceable to his Old World origin—stems from the fear of ghosts and witches of the afterworld. He fears the dead may return as ghosts to plague the living. Therefore, any dead person is a potential danger. Ghosts are believed to take the form of human beings, animals, birds, or whirlwinds, spots of fire, etc. They appear only after dark or at the approach of death. Ghosts may foreshadow general disaster as well as harm to an individual. When a Navaho sees a ghost or dreams of one, it is imperative that the proper ceremony be performed or the individual will surely die. If successful, such ceremonial cures are believed to have killed the witch, one way or another.

Disease and accidental injury are felt to result from an attack by the Holy People, and may be traced to some transgression on the part of a victim. A cure must be effected by a specific chant (a song ceremonial, the songs of which are accompanied by the use of a rattle), and by making sacrificial appeasement to the offended Holy Person, or by engaging the mightier power of a higher divinity to remove the witchery and evil influence of an inferior one. Should a given ceremony fail to cure the sickness, it merely indicates that the offense has not been properly traced and the source must be further sought. Numerous chants may be performed until the patient recovers, or dies. Death is considered to be beyond human calculation. When death of a patient becomes certain, the officiating singer (*xata·łi*), or "medicine man," who conducts a song ceremonial, withdraws before the inevitable.

Chants and Sandpaintings   In general, every chant has its own particular sandpaintings. These represent the divinities or some event connected with a divinity, as told in Navaho legends. More than five hundred different sandpaintings have been recorded, and fifty-eight or more distinct ceremonies—each with its own body of legends. Navaho mythology tells us that originally the drawings were made by the gods, or yé'ii, themselves, and were stitched into some kind of fabric. Actually, it would be more accurate to call these *drypaintings*, for pollen, meal, and other vegetal material, as well as pulverized clay and certain minerals may be used in addition to sand; and occasionally, the paintings are made on buckskin. Usually, the paintings are made on a background of clean sand. The details of the patterns are handed down by memory from one singer to another. Different colors are made by crushing rock, charcoal, or other material into fine powders and mixing them with sand or dirt for easier handling.

Each chant has certain songs, prayers, and herbal medicines which are held to be particularly its own, and the appropriate sandpainting is made inside the hogan where the ceremony is held, or out-of-doors on occasion. But regardless of which chant and paintings are being performed, the basic procedure is the same. Upon completion of the treatment, the patient leaves the hogan, the painting is destroyed in the same order in which it was made, and is deposited to the north of the hogan.

Navaho chants may be grouped according to their mythological associations, rituals they have in common, and as they are addressed to the same or related forces. The six main groups of song ceremonials are: *Blessingway* rites and ceremonials; *War* ceremonials (obsolescent); *Gameway* (hunting) rites (obsolescent); and the three curing ceremonials, *Holyway* employed for the attraction of good, *Evilway* (Ghostway) for exorcism of evil, and *Lifeway* for curing bodily injuries. One of the Holyway curing group, *Beauty-way,* will likely be given if snakes have been offended. If lightning or thunder must be appeased, a *Shootingway* will be used. Where one has trouble from contact with bears, the *Mountain Topway* is the proper treatment. Sometimes a Navaho contracts illness from a non-Navaho, and then he needs to have the *Enemyway* performed. The Enemyway was formerly used in connection with war.

All Navaho rites are accompanied by social functions. One of the features of the Enemyway is the so-called squaw dance. Originally, the intention of this dance was to announce publicly the fact that the girls participating in the ceremony, and who asked the young men to dance with them, were of marriageable age. The young men came to sing and to look over the girls. And crowds gathered to watch the procedure. Today, squaw dances are popular with Indian and non-Indian audiences alike. Groups of Navaho often perform them publicly; and non-Indian people frequently participate. Since the man has to give the girl a present—commonly money—before she will release him from dancing with her, an innocent "victim" may afford the audience much amusement before he "catches on"; and he may accumulate considerable indebtedness to the girl. The squaw dance goes on all night long.

The *Blessingway* places the Navaho in tune with the Holy People. It is performed in approval of a newly selected headman, for an expectant mother, for men going away in their country's service or upon their return. Blessingway songs are sung in the girls' puberty rites and in marriage ceremonies.

Navaho boys and girls are introduced to full participation in ceremonial life by a short initiation rite which is usually held on the next to last night of the *Nightway*. The initiation ceremony and the entire Nightway are popularly known as the *Yeibichei*. The name comes from the principal figures in the initiation ceremony, who represent yé'ii. The Nightway is one of the few Navaho chants that has an attending public dance.

Nightway
(Yeibichei)   The Nightway is a nine-day ceremonial, during which the patient is treated. It is a complex of ceremonies, having a name and an origin legend, carried out according to a certain ritual. Singing occurs for nine nights, sandpaintings are made on the last four days, and prayers and other symbolic offerings and rituals are tendered. On the ninth night comes the climax, a drama illustrating an elaborate myth. The Navaho ride in from far and near, make camp, build their fires, and arrange themselves for the night.

Necessary for the enactment of the Nightway are actors representing certain yé'ii: Talking God (who is also called Yeibichei, "Grandfather of the gods"), Born-of-water, and preferably twelve dancers, representing male and female deities in equal numbers. Monster Slayer, Calling God, Black God, Fringed Mouth, and others may also appear. With these are the singer and the patient.

The dancers impersonating male divinities have their naked torsos, upper extremities, and thighs whitened. Each wears a mask, collar of spruce, loincloth of some showy material, dark wool stockings with red woven garters and moccasins, a silver concha belt with foxskin suspended in the rear, ear pendants, bracelets, and many necklaces of shell, turquois, silver, and coral. In the right hand, each carries a gourd rattle painted white and sometimes decorated with spruce twigs; in the left hand is a spruce twig wand. The casque-shaped mask is painted blue, with a horizontal yellow streak at the bottom crossed by four pairs of perpendicular black lines. A fringe of hair crosses the mask from side to side over the crown of the head. Small eye holes are outlined by red triangles. From the front of the mask, a snout projects; at its base, is a fringe of fur. Two eagle plumes and a bunch of owl feathers are affixed to the mask.

Dancers who impersonate female deities are usually small men or youths. Sometimes women take part; and when they do, they dress in ordinary female costume with which they wear a mask like that of the men. They carry no rattles, but have spruce boughs in each hand. They have no foxskin and wear no blanket; and they dance a different step from that of the men. When men impersonate female deities, they sing in falsetto and wear an ornate kilt or scarf around the hips. Otherwise, they are dressed like the other dancers with whitened body, concha belt with fox skin hanging behind, dark wool stockings and moccasins, ear pendants, necklaces, and bracelets, but in each hand, they carry spruce boughs and their masks are different. The masks cover only the face and throat, and the hair flows free. The masks are nearly square, slightly rounded at the top, painted blue, but with white "ears" protruding at the sides; eye margins are black triangles, and black squares surround the mouth holes; from the bottom of a mask may hang a piece of red cloth, and at the top may be a fringe of short hair. At the center of the top is tied a piece of abalone shell with turkey, eagle, or woodpecker feathers behind it; beads, bits of shell, and other articles of adornment may be added.

The dancers are dressed and painted in the medicine hogan; then they go into an arbor across a cleared area in front of the hogan where they get their masks, wands, and rattles. The performance is in two parts: outside is dancing and singing; within the hogan is chanting, but no dancing.

The visitor will become conscious of soft singing, to the accompaniment of the swishing rhythm of rattles, coming from the hogan. After a time, the performers enter the dancing area. The singer leads the procession. He is followed by Talking God, then the dancers in single file, and Water Sprinkler in the rear. When all are in front of the hogan, the singer turns and faces the others, who halt. The patient, warned by a call, comes from the hogan. Patient and singer then walk along the line of dancers, from west to east. The singer takes meal from a basket carried by the patient and, as they pass each dancer, he sprinkles it on the right arm. Sometimes, the patient takes part in the sprinkling. Patient and singer then turn, sunwise, and retrace their steps to the front of the hogan and face the dancers. The dancers have taken up the sprinkling movements and continue them. Then, with shaking of rattles, and whooping, the dancing and singing get under way.

Born-of-water serves as clown. While the others are dancing, he engages in all sorts of capers, getting in their way, sometimes imitating Talking God, losing some item of attire and making a great to-do about it, dancing, and acting as buffoon in general.

Throughout the night, different acts are performed in an orderly and regular manner. The participants take short rest periods. It is said the most desirable number of repetitions of the dance is forty-eight, when four sets of dancers perform twelve times each. But many variations from the standard may be seen. After the dancers have finished their last song, singers inside the hogan chant the four Finishing Hymns; one or more assistants may aid the singer, sitting at his right. Those who are near the hogan may hear this singing, but few white people are privileged to witness the ceremony within a medicine lodge. As the last verse is sung, the singer overturns an inverted basket drum toward the west, making movements as though releasing winged insects from under the basket and driving them out through the smoke hole in the roof; he blows a breath after the invisible insects as they supposedly depart. During this song, an assistant to the singer has been applying meal to the lower jaw of the patient. Finally, an act of unraveling the drumstick is performed. While an assistant carries out this procedure, the singer gives final instructions to the patient. All are then free to depart. Certain taboos must be observed and definite rites followed. The patient must not go to sleep before sunset. The singer retires to the medicine hogan to sleep and must do so for four consecutive nights. (Matthews 1902)

Mountain Topway The Mountain Topway—commonly known as the Mountain Chant—is usually held over nine consecutive days. The first four days are not of particular interest to the general visitor. On the fifth day, in conjunction with the curative rites, the first sandpainting is made in the hogan. Other paintings are made on the three succeeding days. On the ninth day, preparation goes forward for the nighttime ceremonies—the making of plumed arrows, wands, trees, and so forth. The final night is the big spectacle. A great woodpile is surrounded by a huge corral with an opening to the east. It is made of evergreen branches. As this corral is being finished—just after sunset—the head singer stands at the entrance, singing and shaking his rattle. As night falls, the Navaho spectators enter the sacred enclosure, build their small fires near the confining wall and settle themselves to watch the night's performances.

When the great bonfire is roaring, a warning whistle is heard from the outer darkness. A dozen lithe, lean men come bounding into the corral. They wear only breechclouts and moccasins. Their bodies are painted white. They carry feather-tipped wands which they wave to the four directions as they move around the fire. The heat is terrific, but they circle it twice. Then, they plunge toward the flames, close enough to burn the plumes from the ends of their wands. The next feat is for each to restore the feathers to his wands.

Because of this startling spectacle at the beginning, this ceremony is frequently called the fire dance. A dozen or so dances may follow—each with its chorus of male singers. Acts such as arrow swallowing, growing of the yucca plant, feathers dancing in a basket, and other skillful legerdemain may be performed. Very elaborate costumes are worn.

The final act in this ceremony is another fire dance around the renewed fire. Before the dancers appear, strange sounds are heard in the distance—the blowing of horns and shrill calls. As the sounds come closer, perhaps ten men advance through the eastern entryway into the corral. They wear only narrow loincloths and moccasins, and their bodies are covered with white clay, giving them a ghostly appearance. Each man, except the leader, carries a long, thick bundle of shredded juniper bark in each hand; and one carries an extra bundle for the leader to use later. The leader carries four small fagots of flaming juniper bark. All dance around the great central fire four times, waving their bundles toward the fire. On the east side, they halt; the leader advances toward the fire, kindles one of the fagots, shouts loudly, and tosses it over the east wall of the corral. Then, they move around to the south, the west, and the north, where similar acts are performed. But before the leader throws the burning brand to the north, he lights the bark bundles of the other dancers.

The entire group begins to dance wildly about the roaring fire. They run hither and yon, the breeze fanning the brands into long brilliant streamers of flame, which play upon the bodies of the participants. As the bundles burn, glowing fragments drop off; these are tossed about or thrown upon the other dancers. Every time a brand is applied to the flesh of one of the performers, the trumpeting sound is heard. The juniper bundles are relighted from the central fire in case they cease to burn. When a brand finally is consumed, the dancer drops the ash and runs out of the corral. One by one, they all disappear. (Mathews 1887)

The fire dies; dawn comes. Three more openings are broken in the corral wall. The Indians pick up their blankets and fire-blackened coffee pots, mount horses or pile into wagons or motor vehicles, and head for home. By the time the sun is well over the horizon, the cars are out of sight, but the horses and wagons are still drawing crooked lines across the countryside.

The fire dance is frequently performed alone at public exhibitions, such as at ceremonial events in Gallup, the Flagstaff Pow-wow, and similar exhibitions, where it makes a dramatic climax to an evening's program.

Most of the Navaho chants can be held at any time of the year, but the curing ceremonials are restricted to certain months. The Nightway and the Mountain Topway cannot be given until after the first killing frost; they are usually held in November and December. The Enemyway is generally performed after completion of the spring work and before the harvesting and marketing season arrives.

The Ramah Navaho (*see* pp. 110-12) do not hold some of the longer chants, such as the Nightway and Mountain Topway, but many of the shorter ceremonials are performed frequently. Local practitioners—who include singers, curers, prayer makers, diagnosticians, and witches—know about twenty different ceremonials. Around twenty adult men are classed as practitioners, but most of these are curers, who know only part of a ceremonial, as opposed to singers who know at least one ceremonial of five or more nights' duration. (*See* Vogt 1951:17) All who practice any form of divination are known as diagnosticians, "those who investigate to reveal." (Kluckhohn and Wyman 1940:15-16) A dozen or so of the Ramah men and women are diagnosticians.

Cost of ceremonials is borne by the patient or by his family. Today, that means as much as seven hundred dollars or more for a Yeibichei, and four hundred dollars for a squaw dance. A Yeibichei singer receives from seventy-five dollars to one hundred and fifty dollars in cash, plus one hundred dollars to two hundred dollars worth of goods, and small contributions from people going in to witness the sandpaintings. For a squaw dance, the singer may get twenty-five dollars for preparations and procedural instructions, plus a possible additional take from contributions during the ceremony. Those assisting the singer are also paid. Equipment such as baskets, herbs, deer skins, and the like, must be purchased. And, most important of all, those who attend the ceremonial must be fed. Thus, all Navaho ceremonials are expensive undertakings.

The Peyote Cult   During the difficult times that prevailed in the 1930's, the peyote cult gained a foothold among the Navaho and some of the other Southwestern Indians. Peyote, a hallucinogenic cactus, had been widely used among Mexican Indians in religious rites since prehistoric times. Spanish documents mention it early in the seventeenth century. Until the 1800's, peyote was eaten by Indian peoples privately to induce visions or as a trance-producing feature of group dancing. Then, toward the end of the nineteenth century, use of peyote became the core of a new ceremonial complex among the Indians of Oklahoma; it was highly developed by the Kiowa and spread to other Indians who used peyote in various rites.

In 1918, a number of the Indian peoples in Oklahoma incorporated a movement known as the Native American Church; peyote served as the means of spiritual communion between man and his deity—known to the Navaho as *pioniyo*. The Navaho, around 1940, began to practice the peyote cult with increasing vigor. They learned the peyote ceremony from the Ute Indians of southern Colorado, who are said to have used peyote for years.

In 1944, the name was changed to the "Native American Church of the United States," and in 1955, it was changed again, to the "Native American Church of North America," to include Canadian peyote groups. (Anonymous 1970a:12)

For a long time, the use of peyote by the Navaho was "an underground phenomenon, illegal by tribal law, the subject of fierce, though carefully hushed, controversy. Now, it is said to be surfacing as one of the Navaho's most significant cultural crutches in a troubled time. The cult displays a unique blending of traditional Navaho ceremonialism, fundamentalist Christian elements, and 'pan-Indian moral principles' " (Nabokov 1969:129*); it appears to be meeting the deepest spiritual needs of a transitional people. Estimates of the practicing Navaho membership in the Four Corners region run from one-third to 80 per cent.

The increase of peyotism seems due, largely, to the introduction of new and varied doctrines by missionaries of differing Christian denominations. In the majority of instances, the result was a partial Christianization, which left the Navaho (and other Indian groups) with a sense of insecurity regarding their traditional religion. One investigator, who made an in-depth survey at mission stations on the Navaho reservation, found that "a good deal of Christian mission work completely missed the idea that religion is involved in the whole life for any people who have come out of animism," as have the Navaho. It was noted that the Native American Church has positive values in its favor, for example, emphasis on family life and stress on fellowship. The investigator stated that, "Despite twenty-five years of work, and considerable expenditure, mission work for the church I was studying had made an unsatisfactory impact." (*See* Thrapp 1967-II:6)

Before the peyote cult reached the Navaho, nothing seemed to bridge the gap between the old ceremonial ways and the new patterns resulting from culture changes and the demands of the modern world. More and more, the ills which formerly called forth a singer to perform a Navahoway, or a curing ceremony, came to be met by Peyote Road rites.

A recent participant in a Navaho peyote ceremony has stated that peyote (*Lophophora williamsii*) when eaten, produces "relatively standard physiological effects, but markedly varying psychological ones, depending on the user's cultural background." He explains that:

Peyote's make-up of alkaloids—at least 15 at latest count, the most studied being mescaline—acts like a series of timed depth charges. First comes an unpleasant, stomach-unsettling sensation. Within a half-hour this dies, leaving a face starting to flush, pupils dilating, salivation increasing and a sense of exhilaration growing through the body, resembling the effect of swift intakes of pure oxygen. Then one moves into a period of withdrawal, of intense color awareness, of successions of hallucinations when eyes are closed, energies focused inward.

A few hours later, this levels off onto an intense plateau. Then whatever one is prompted to concentrate upon—here the cultural situation is a critical determinant—becomes uncannily luminous. During these hours, reflexes are heightened, occasional muscle twitching is common, time is overestimated, spacial perception is altered, hearing and sight yield intensified tones, ideas flow rapidly, but physical movement is awkward.

This final period . . . diminishes through the following day with no aftereffects . . . ." (Nabokov 1969:30*)

The performance of rites of the Peyote Road is a dusk-to-dawn affair which is conducted by an officiating priest known as the Road Chief. He is assisted by three other principals: a Drummer Chief who does much of the drumming, the Cedar Chief who sprinkles powdered juniper ("cedar") on the fire during the meeting, and a Fire Chief. With "Indian sage," the Road Chief prepares an altar on the floor of a hogan, shredding the sage while the Fire Chief, who sits on the north side of the door, tends the fire built in the center of the chamber of uniformly split wood. The sticks are arranged in V-shape, and flames rise upward from the tip. Then, the Road Chief arranges a nest of sage pods in the middle of the altar which he has fashioned in a crescent of earth known as the Peyote Moon. A large peyote blossom is carefully placed in the sage bed, representing the Peyote Chief, symbol of the spiritual medium of the Peyote Road.

After the altar has been prepared, the participants take the sacramental food, munching on peyote buds that have been sliced and dried, or sipping brewed "tea" made therefrom. The final period of effectiveness is entered toward midnight. Then, the Road Chief readies a kettle drum, inside of which are a few soaked coals and water "to 'strengthen' the drumbeats." The religious services then begin—a night of ceremonial praying, smoking, and singing, of confessing and weeping, which continue until dawn. Then, a traditional blessing of the peyote breakfast occurs, followed by a final prayer.

Such ceremonies take place on Thanksgiving eve and the night before Christmas and the New Year, at Easter, the Fourth of July, and on Armed Forces Day.

Insignia of the peyote cult consist of a cardinal red tie and socks, silver "water bird" ornament, and a rectangular box made of

*© 1969 by The New York Times Company. Reproduced by permission.

"cedar" for ritual paraphernalia—feathered fans, drum, eagle bone whistle, gourd rattles with beaded handles, and a horsehair-tipped staff. As one travels through Navaholand, the decals he sees with the letters "N.A.C." and a spread-wing bird motif affixed to car or truck windows indicate membership in the Native American Church.

State and federal laws are in conflict and confusion regarding the legality of use of peyote. A bill permitting the use of peyote for bona fide religious purposes was passed by the New Mexico Legislature in 1956. Four years later, the state of Arizona decreed peyote use legal for NAC members, and a few other states have taken similar action; federal tolerance of its ritual use depends largely upon a Supreme Court ruling of 1961.

It is recorded that: "On October 9, 1967, the Navajo Tribal Council adopted a declaration of basic Navajo rights which cancelled all previous laws denying freedom of religion inconsistent with this declaration."

Title 17, subchapter 21, section 641, of the Navajo Tribal Code, in re "sale, use or possession" of peyote, states:

It shall be unlawful for any person to transport peyote into Navajo country or buy, sell, possess or use peyote in any form, and any person convicted of violating this provision shall be guilty of a misdemeanor punishable by a fine not to exceed $100 or imprisonment not to exceed nine months or both; provided that it shall not be unlawful for any member of the Native American Church to transport peyote into Navajo country, or buy, sell, possess or use peyote in any form, in connection with the religious practices, sacraments or services of the Native American Church. (Anonymous 1970a:12)

The Navaho, like all other Americans, have been beset by the barrage of capitalized initials that are poured continually into governmental nomenclature, the news media, and everyday speech. Much of the time, those outside a particular organization have little or no concept of what various initials may denote. Then, when the Navaho, or others, select initials to indicate certain committees, groups, agencies, operations, and the like in their *own* language, the uninitiated are indeed perplexed. (Yes, the Navaho language has now been fully recorded, as set forth by Young). (Young 1961:430-500)

One reading periodicals, viewing TV, or listening to radios which report happenings in the Southwest frequently sees or hears comments on DNA. These initials are seldom explained. And small wonder. They refer to *Dinebeiina Nahiilna be Agaditahe*, Navaho for the Office-of-Economic-Opportunity-financed "Attorneys who contribute to the revitalization of the people." (Anonymous 1970g)

OFF-RESERVATION
NAVAHO GROUPS

Ramah Navaho

Not only visitors in the Southwest, but residents of New Mexico as well, are often surprised to learn that several groups of Navaho Indians have lands located away from the main reservation. The largest of these is the *Ramah Navaho*, numbering 1,380, of whom 1,075 reside in the community. Their land lies southeast of Ramah, New Mexico, both north and south of El Morro National Monument on State Highway 53, a few miles east of the pueblo of Zuñi. This is a belt approximately eighteen by thirty miles in extent, with elevation averaging around 7,000 feet, but ranging up to 9,000 feet in the mountains, where good hunting is offered. Although there are deep canyons to the north, most of the region consists of broad valleys covered with grass or sagebrush bordered by ridges forested with piñon and juniper. Nearly five hundred different kinds of plants have been identified in the area, and the Navaho knew the names of all but three of these. (*See* Vestal 1952)

Some of the Navaho and also a number of Apaches managed to escape from Fort Sumner during their exile. We are told that among the Navaho escapees were the parents of a man known as Many Beads, who went to live among the Chiricahua Apache. Many Beads had a son who was born among the Chiricahua and was but two years old when the Navaho captives began their trek back from captivity. Learning of this movement, the lad's parents also set forth for their old homeland. After a winter spent at Acoma, the family settled in the mountains near Fort Wingate. There they were joined by Many Beads, who accompanied them back to a place where they had dwelt formerly, at a spring near present Ramah (where Mormon missionaries in 1876 persuaded the Navaho to allow them to establish a small colony—which, in spite of a severe smallpox epidemic, was refounded in 1882 and has grown into a community of several hundred people). Another Navaho and his mother lived there likewise, and thus, we know of the two families in that locality about 1876; undoubtedly, others settled there, for the released captives strongly tended to return to their former homesites. The son of Many Beads became a patriarch of the community and longtime leader. (*See* Young 1968:43)

The Ramah Navaho have a political structure with characteristics of a band. It has long had a single headman. Through time, a number of factions have developed, following the conservative and progressive pattern of so many Indian groups. The former wish to continue their old ways, while the latter favor the ways of the white man. Of the total of 146,996 acres under control of the Ramah group, less than 200 acres are farmed, and livestock is grazed. In most ways, the ceremonial structure follows that of the other Navaho.

The people of the community constitute the Ramah Chapter; this has a president, and an elected delegate to the Navajo Tribal Council.

For their education, about one hundred youngsters of this Navaho group ride buses from their homes to the Ramah public school. For 148, dormitory space has been provided so that students can live in Ramah. The dormitory system operates in a modern facility consisting of four separate buildings that are divided into sections and attractively decorated; the grounds are well landscaped. Each building houses a different age group and sex. In January, 1970, the staff numbered twenty-seven being comprised mostly of Navaho and Zuñi people trained in the problems of children.

Although the Navaho long opposed the dormitory idea because it took the youngsters away from home, they came to realize the benefits not possible in the scattered, dirt-floor hogans: good food regularly served, running water, children and toys with which to play, as well as education.

Each section of the dorm consists of a room divided into sleeping quarters, a lounge area with television and desks, and a recreation area. The children sleep in bunk beds and each shares a dresser with another child. Each one performs a daily chore, attends classes and studies; otherwise, time is free to do as one wishes. Tutors are available to assist those having difficulties with their studies.

In addition to some four hundred school-age Navaho who do not live in the dorm or come to Ramah by bus, one hundred others ride a bus to the Fence Lake School; a few attend the school at Fort Wingate or the Intermountain School at Brigham City, Utah; and several go to school in Salt Lake City. In 1970, one hundred and twenty were enrolled in the Albuquerque Indian School. It is planned that more school and dormitory buildings will be built in Ramah.

Some years ago, a fine school building was constructed there and equipped for students of high school grades, the Gallup-McKinley County High School. Then, in 1968, the plant was abandoned and allowed to fall into disrepair. The students were sent by bus to schools in Zuñi or towns miles distant, and frequently to boarding schools in California, Utah or Oklahoma. The Ramah Navaho fought this action effectively and set about to establish a school of their own. Funds were secured from the BIA, OEO, and from private foundations.

The Ramah school board was incorporated in February, 1970, and a summer session was opened in June. The school board involved the Navaho people of the district; and the summer project brought a Neighborhood Youth Corps into the picture. Living in tents, the students started work aided by adult Navaho workmen from Ramah. A new roof was placed on the old school building and general repairs were made. The students entered into the creation of courses for their school; students and their parents were polled to determine what the people closest to the school felt it should offer. Then only was a teaching staff hired, a staff of broad and varied backgrounds. It is felt that upon being graduated from this high school, the young people should be able to understand and participate in Navaho culture, "be employable, and be able to go to college if they choose." (Bartel 1970:2B; Waliczek 1970) A number of vocational and cultural areas considered to be a part of the school's curriculum have been stressed. The director was to be a Navaho, and the initial non-Indian personnel to be replaced by qualified Indians.

The Edward Elliott Foundation of New York helped fund the summer school, and officers of the foundation are deeply impressed by the efforts of the Navaho to control their own school.

The Puertocito (Alamo) Navaho   Next in size of the off-reservation groups is the *Puertocito Navaho*, a band that has been separated from the main body for some one hundred-odd years. This group developed in part from Navaho slaves who ran away from their Spanish masters living in Socorro. They congregated at Alamo, or "at Field's place," about thirty-five miles northwest of Magdalena, New Mexico; from this location, they are commonly called the "Alamo Navaho." It is said that they were once part of the "enemy Navaho," and that they are called *Tsa Dei'alth*, or "stone chewers," for, when they fought, they got so angry that they chewed rocks. (*See* Harrington 1940:515-516)

The few who settled in the Field locality intermarried with Chiricahua and Mescalero Apaches and with Mexicans; they were joined by Navaho from other areas, some of whom fled there to escape Kit Carson, and others who fled from Fort Sumner. Between 1912 and 1920, allotments were made to these Puertocito Navaho, and purchased lands were added to their holdings by the federal government and the Navaho tribe. Their domain now embraces some 56,670 acres, and their population is about 920. The land is semiarid, with many deep arroyos and high mesas. Grass is in limited supply among the piñon and juniper growth.

In 1941, a day school was built and opened for the Alamo youngsters. Teachers did not like the isolation and student attendance was irregular; as a result, the school failed. A survey made in 1959 revealed the average adult education to be one and a half years. That year, a dormitory was opened at Magdalena so students could live there and attend the public schools. The graveled road to Magdalena was improved; otherwise, country roads and dim trails must be followed over the reservation.

Until the early 1960's, almost everyone lived in log-built hogans. Then, a house-building project was initiated and now most of the Navaho families have moved into new homes. Each faces the east, as do traditional hogans. In 1967, a Rural Electrification Administration power line was brought to the reservation, enabling the people to have modern appliances for the first time. The main water source, Alamo Springs, was improved and the beginnings of a running water system was started.

The political structure follows that of the main reservation. (*See* Euler 1961)

The Cañoncito Navaho

A third group, which lives some twenty-five miles west from Albuquerque, a few miles north of Interstate Highway I-40, is known as the *Dine'é Ana'i*, or "enemy Navaho." They derive from Navaho who had moved southwestward into the Cebolleta Mountains under Spanish pressure during the eighteenth century, and they remained there when the main body of Navaho moved to the west. Then, as those who had been confined at Fort Sumner trekked back toward their homeland, Chief Delgadito separated about four hundred people from the seven thousand who left Fort Sumner on 15 June 1868—fifteen days after the Treaty of 1868 was signed. These returned to their old territory in the Cebolleta region. Later, remnants of Sandoval's Cebolleta band received allotments and other lands in what came to be known as the Cañoncito reservation. Since those earlier days, other Navaho have married into the community. Today, they number close to 1,125. Their land holdings total 76,813 acres.

In 1969, the Cañoncito group initiated an annual rodeo. This is scheduled around the middle of July, and may follow a horse sale. The rodeo features bareback riding and bull riding, calf roping, team roping, and barrel racing. Winners of each event, based on average points, receive awards. Refreshments are sold.

Each of these off-reservation groups lives in accordance with the general pattern of Navaho culture. They all engage in farming and stock raising. Few arts are practiced; certain Cañoncito women make fine fabric dolls with characteristic adornments, and they fashion attractive beaded ornaments. A limited number of baskets are made by the Ramah Navaho.

The "Checkerboard Area" In addition to the above off-reservation peoples, about 25,000 Navaho live in the so-called "checkerboard area." This extends eastward from the Navaho reservation to the Jicarilla Apache reservation, and south of that beyond the town of Cuba. Here the public domain (662,776 acres) has been allotted so that each alternate square mile is Indian land, with non-Indian sections in between—hence the designation checkerboard. The normal allotment to an Indian is 160 acres. The Eastern Navajo School has been built south of Huerfano Mesa—a modern community near the Blanco Trading Post—and that area is called the Eastern Navajo District by the government officers at Crown Point.

GREAT WIDE BEAUTIFUL

that's how I describe the Apache land
on which I live.
You see, I'm an Apache
living around wonderful rivers, grass and cactus.
I will long remember the times I had
with my mother when we walked across fields
among the dancing flowers. With a mother around
every joy is here.
We went through places where long ago
my people once lived
and now it is deserted
with trees, weeds, growing here and there.
Mountains are on all sides blue, green mixed together,
which makes a pretty color. . . .
And before us was a river flowing
and alongside it were grasses, trees
dancing among the breeze: then. . . .
Slowly we started home in the direction
where the sun was setting.
This place which I call home is really my home
and I hope it always will be.

By Lenora Palmer (White Mountain Apache)

From: *Art and Indian Children.* Curriculum Bulletin No. 7, 1970. Institute of American Indian Arts, Santa Fe, N. M.

.... THE APACHE INDIANS

BRIEF HISTORY   The Apache peoples spread southward, as Athabascan bands, along the easternside of the Rocky Mountains. Each local group had a headman, who led by reason of prestige and good example, and a headwoman, whose function was to council her people in the ways of living, and especially to organize wild food-gathering parties among the women.

Our data on the Apaches have come mostly from documentary accounts written by non-Indians and from ethnological studies. It was said that the Apache dwellings were similar to the forked-stick hogan, and they had many culture traits akin to those of the Navaho of the Gobernador Phase. In their migrations, they picked up numerous Plains Indian characteristics, such as the type of dwellings (tipi), articles of attire and hair styles, and perhaps, elementary knowledge of horticulture.

Not a great deal has been known about the Apaches archaeologically, although the late Carl Lumholtz is said to have dug some sites in Chihuahua, Mexico, about the turn of the twentieth century (*See* Lister 1958 and Lumholtz 1902) and certain investigators have engaged in local studies (*See* Gerald 1958; Gunnerson 1960; 1969a; Gunnerson and Gunnerson 1970; 1971a, 1971b) These latter works have revealed that: "For two centuries or more, many Apaches were peaceful farmers, living in permanent villages on the eastern edge of the American Southwest and in the central and southern plains." In the Southwest, these Apaches "rapidly learned a new way of life that included dependence upon corn. They manufactured pottery, and constructed houses more permanent than the skin tepees in which they had originally lived." Working along the eastern base of the Sangre de Cristo mountain range, near Cimarron and Las Vegas, New Mexico, in 1967, the archaeologists made an exciting discovery; they uncovered a seven-room adobe dwelling that had been built around 1700 by the Jicarilla Apache, in Pueblo manner. (*See* Gunnerson 1969a)

The cultural material associated with the house structures indicated extensive trade with the Pueblos and western Texas peoples. The Apache evidently went on bison hunting expeditions. At another site, evidence was found of a type of dwelling not previously identified with the Apache—a circular pit about twelve feet in diameter and two feet deep, which had had a rock wall laid

42

Fig. 1   A Navaho singer in characteristic attire. He wears a
shell-disc and turquois necklace and a die-stamped and
embossed concho belt and has a bowguard (*kehto*) on his left
wrist. His hair is arranged chongo style and held in place by a
colorful kerchief. Across his chest is a hand-tanned band
supporting a quiver, which is worn at the back; these are
commonly fashioned from mountain lion skin. A bow extends
from the quiver.

Photo from Elita Wilson Collection

Fig. 2 A Navaho summer home in Monument Valley, with the family living near their fields.

Photo courtesy Laura Gilpin, Santa Fe

Fig. 3 Apache and Navaho Indians under guard constructing barracks at Fort Sumner (Bosque Redondo), 1864-1865. They were paid $0.25 per day for their labor, and keep was provided.

Photo courtesy Museum of New Mexico, John Gaw Meem Collection

Fig. 4 These Navaho twins were born at Fort Sumner during the time their parents were being held there, but they survived through all the vicissitudes that the Navaho experienced, and they were living on the reservation at the time of the centennial observances in 1968. When the Long Walk was reenacted, these two rode along part of the way on one of the wagons.

Photo courtesy Navajo Tribal Museum

Figs. 5-13 Navaho women and girls in styles of dress commonly worn during the past century. Many carry articles that signify their respective skills and household tasks. Photographed at the time of the centennial observance of the Navaho Nation's return from the Long Walk and captivity of Fort Sumner.

Photos courtesy Navaho Tribal Museum

Figs. 14-22 Navaho men and boys who participated in the centennial activities commemorating the Long Walk to Bosque Redondo at Fort Sumner and the century of progress since 1868. The pictures show typical clothing worn during the century, including some accoutrements used especially on significant cultural occasions.

Photos courtesy Navaho Tribal Museum

Fig. 23   Black-robed friars and others mounted on horses, rayed circular elements, and various examples of Navaho art at Canyon del Muerto, Arizona.

Photo by B. P. Dutton

Fig. 24   A Navaho singer and his assistants making a sand-painting in the hogan of a patient who is being treated with a Nightway ceremonial for an illness.

Photo courtesy Laura Gilpin, Santa Fe

Fig. 25 Gáhan dancers representing the supernatural Mountain Topway Spirits. Note the
type of drum and drumstick
used.

Photo by Elita Wilson

Fig. 26 A Black Mountain Navaho dance group, performers
of the Mountaintop Way at a ceremonial observance at Gallup,
New Mexico.

Photo by Elita Wilson

Fig. 27   An eagle dance, performed in the plaza at Laguna.

Photo by B. P. Dutton

up around it and roofed over. Spanish contact materials were found there. A large site near Las Vegas exhibited more of the ringed construction. Some 250 rings of rocks appeared to have been used to hold down the bottoms of tipis. There, residence was less permanent, and this indicates a shifting from location on the valley floors to low terraces (reflecting a need for more protection from unfriendly peoples, such as the Comanche). Trade items in these villages appear to date in the nineteenth century. (*See* Anonymous 1967)

In 1969 and 1970, investigations were made at the ruins of Pecos, for the pueblo had been an important trading center for Pueblo-Plains Indians in the late 1600's and early 1700's, and probably long before. Within the confines of the Pecos National Monument, nine areas were found that yielded Apache pottery. Other sites in the area will be discovered with further investigating.

The historical Apache were known as notable enemies whose hardihood was incredible. Meat was the favorite food, and where available, mescal was harvested and eaten in great quantities. When necessary, the Apache literally could "live off the land," eating berries, roots, seeds, cactus, or crawling animals (but never fish, or snakes—which they feared—or turkeys and dogs that ate them). They were extremely healthy before European diseases were introduced, and could go practically naked in zero weather.

Characteristically, the Apache has a splendid physique. Although individuals vary greatly, the people average above medium height. The well-formed head rests on a short muscular neck. The face is broad, with high cheekbones and strong nose. Apache men have rather sparse beards which they formerly plucked.

Little girls were given the same training as boys. Every day, they practiced with bow and arrows, slings and spears. They were taught to mount an unsaddled horse without help, and to ride expertly. At puberty, Apache youths were tested in all kinds of hardships by their elders. Girls went through extensive rites, of which more is written below.

The Apache men have high regard for their women; in days of old, particularly, they were respected, cherished, and protected. Chastity was rigidly enforced. Children were seldom spaced closer than four years. In times of warfare, wives were permitted to go on the warpath with their husbands. With the Apache, scalping was not a custom; they abhorred mutilation. When death occurred, sympathy was not extended by words. A killing obliged the next of kin to seek revenge. Great store was set by promises, and a liar was despised by all. The Apache felt that "without respect no human relationship (was) of any value." (Ball 1970:29)

Essentially, the Apache were a mountain people, traveling from ridge to ridge, but they were at home equally in the parched semidesert wastes by which they were surrounded; they were hunting and fighting people. As one writer has said summarily:

> They moved about freely, wintering on the Río Grande or farther south, ranging the buffalo plains in the summer, always following the sun and the food supply. They owned nothing and everything. They did as they pleased and bowed to no man. Their women were chaste. Their leaders kept their promises. They were mighty warriors who depended on success in raiding for wealth and honor. To their families they were kind and gentle, but they could be unbelievably cruel to their enemies—fierce and revengeful when they felt that they had been betrayed. (Sonnichsen 1958:4)

They became primarily tipi-dwellers. Those who lived in the forested dells in the mountains erected shelters fashioned of slender poles which were covered with brush and grass—the wickiup. Two general types of these were used: one built on a tipi frame, and the true dome-shaped *wickiup*. Each was built with doorway toward the east. Adopting matrilineal descent, the Apache also took over matrilocal residence as a social pattern. (*See* Kaut 1957:39) Band exogamy was not required, but marriages between kinsmen were forbidden. A girl's mother and other female relatives constructed a dwelling for a newly married couple, not far distant from the maternal abode. The mother-in-law taboo is observed, and cousins of the opposite sex are not supposed to talk directly; they should have some sort of a screen between, or at least have their backs to each other. Kinship is reckoned bilaterally.

Rather than shaking hands, or kissing, as is common in many cultures, Apaches embrace upon meeting one another. The Apache is very modest, and the privacy of others is highly respected.

THE CHIRICAHUA AND MESCALERO

The Chiricahua and Mescalero Apaches are closely related, and they formerly occupied adjacent areas. It is commonly said that the Chiricahua territory lay to the west of the Río Grande, centering around Ojo Caliente, or Warm Springs, the water of which seeps from the foot of a little hill on the west side of the San Mateo range, north of Monticello, New Mexico; from there, bands, numbering around one thousand persons in all, ranged through southwestern New Mexico and southeastern Arizona, and over the northern parts of Sonora and Chihuahua in Mexico. By the seventeenth century, they were strongly entrenched in those regions and fighting to retain them.

More details have been given recently by Jámes Kaywaykla, an Apache who was born near Warm Springs and who died in 1963 at the age of about ninety years. Early writers included the Warm Springs Apaches as Chiricahua, but Kaywaykla has said that the Apaches themselves recognized four bands; of these, only the groups headed by Cochise and by Chihuahua were true Chiricahua.

In the words of Kaywaykla, "Juh was chief of the *Nednhi* Apaches, whose stronghold was in the Sierra Madre of Mexico (their "Blue Mountains"). Gerónimo was leader, but not chief of the *Bedonkohes*, whose territory was around the headwaters of the Gila. Though closely associated, we were distinct groups." The Warm Springs Apache in their own tongue were *Chihinne*, or "Red People," so called because of a band of red clay which was painted across their faces. (Ball 1970: xiv)*

The band was the political unit, with leader and followers. This system had no tribal chief, no council of leaders, and no device for decision making. The bands were not local groups; "they were not resource holding units, and exercised no control over a specific portion of land." (Basehart 1970:92) For another thing, bands "grew, lost members, disappeared, and new groups developed," resulting in "a continual but gradual redistribution of the population." (Basehart 1970:93) This was difficult for the white officials to comprehend; they needed some or fixed point of reference.

If a band was small, the members usually formed a single scattered encampment; larger bands might have several camps. The core of a band was a "relative group," primarily—but not necessarily—kinsmen.

The Apache women of these bands wore two-piece dresses made of calico; skirts were long and full, and long blouses were worn outside of the skirt belts. Each woman carried a knife, and some had ammunition belts and rifles. Apache girls had their hair arranged around two willow hoops, worn over the ears. Some of the older women dressed their hair in Plains Indian manner, parted in the middle, with two braids. The attire for warriors consisted of calico shirt, a muslin breechclout supported by a belt, one or more

---

In the Days of Victorio: Recollections of a Warm Springs Apache, James K. Kaywaykla, Narrator, by Eve Ball, Tucson: University of Arizona Press, copyright 1970. All quotations reproduced by permission.

cartridge belts, moccasins, and a headband to keep their long hair out of the eyes. To distinguish themselves, the Warm Springs people wore a band of buckskin, colored yellow with sacred pollen of cattails, over the right shoulder and tied to the belt under the left arm. Buckskin shirts and beaded robes of the women were used for ceremonial attire. Blankets, too, were used. Some men wore large, loose deerskin coats in winter.

The moccasins had high tops that could be drawn up for warmth, or could be folded below the knee for protection against thorns and rock. Kaywaykla has said: "In those folds we carried our valuable possessions, valuable primarily in the sense of usefulness. Sometimes these included extra cowhide soles, for soles wore out quickly and had to be replaced. We carried the endthorns of a mescal plant with fiber attached for sewing the soles to the uppers. The soles were tanned with the hair left on, and they projected beyond the toes and terminated in a circular flap with a metal button sewed to the center. This piece turned back over the toes for additional protection. Because we frequently had to abandon our horses to scale cliffs, the moccasin was our most important article of dress." (Ball 1970:17-18)

In Kaywaykla's youth, Victorio (who succeeded Mangas Coloradas, after Cuchillo Negro had been leader for a time) was their chief; among the notable leaders were Nana and Loco, et al. Leaders were men of influence rather than wielders of power.

When the U.S.A. assumed sovereignty over New Mexico in 1848, the Mescalero utilized the country to the east of the Río Grande, extending from northern Mexico to the region south of Santa Fe; a branch dwelt on the plains in western Texas. Natziti was the head chief, a contemporary of Victorio. The Apaches all knew their territory intimately; they had no specially built strongholds but survived by ranging rapidly in and out of wild, rugged places. When they camped, they never stayed close to the edge of a water body, for "the water belonged to all creatures, not man alone." They selected a campsite in a grassy location or a wooded area and carried water from the source to the camp.

Horses were well cared for, never ridden to death. The Apache did not travel at night, nor did they fight during the nighttime unless forced to do so by soldiers or others.

Harassment and encroachment by the Spaniards, conflicts with the Comanche during the latter part of the eighteenth century, then Mexican domination and the American occupation of the mid-1800's with its increasing pressures and controls; such vicissitudes were more than these free souls could accept. Their original friendliness toward foreigners ceased. Striving to hold their ancestral lands, their life ways, and their very lives brought forth the fierce emotions of the Apache. Naturally, they raided the newcomers' settlements and drove off their animals—especially horses, mules, and burros, which increased their mobility and speeded their getaway. They killed when it seemed necessary, and came to be the most dreaded warriors of the Southwest.

As the westward expansion of the white men heightened, the Apache were pushed from their holdings and the game upon which they depended was driven away. Having no place to go, they turned southward into Mexico, from where raids were made across the border. After the Mexican and U.S. governments combined efforts to quell the Apaches, life for them became extremely perilous.

In 1863, about four hundred Mescalero Apache were taken to the concentration camp, Bosque Redondo or Fort Sumner, on the Pecos River. (*See* McNitt 1970) Colonel Carleton planned to put all of the Apaches there . . . and make farmers of them! When the Navaho, enemies of the Apaches, were rounded up and confined there, too, the situation became unendurable. Smallpox contracted by the Navaho from the soldiers contaminated the water being used by the Mescalero. Seeing the Navaho dying by the hundreds, the Mescalero took what they could carry and fled to one of their old campsites on the Bonito, above Fort Stanton—which had been established in 1855.

Victorio outwitted Colonel Carleton and kept his band from being sent to Bosque Redondo. By an Executive Order in 1870, the government promised him a permanent reservation for his Chihinne band at Warm Springs. The decimated group assembled there, and an adobe building was erected for their headquarters across the Cañada Alamosa from Warm Springs.

At the same time, Cochise, the Chiricahua chief, who had gathered his band near Warm Springs, was to have a reservation about his stronghold. Neither promise was kept. As a result, Cochise resumed raiding. In 1872, the Chiricahua were separated from the Mescalero by establishment of reservations for each group.

Because another Executive Order had come through, returning the Warm Springs (Chiricahua) reservation to the public domain, Victorio was commanded to move his people to a high mountain valley of the Tularosa River in westernmost New Mexico—a place impossible during the winter. Severe cold, starvation, and death forced the government agent to let the Apache return to Warm Springs for a short time. Other leaders, including Gerónimo, brought their bands to camp in the vicinity.

During 1877, Gerónimo had been joined by bands of Apaches from Mexico, and numerous raids were made in southern New Mexico and Arizona. Victorio received orders from the agent at San Carlos to come there and bring his people. For their compliance, all of the leaders were arrested. Gerónimo and seven other headmen were already there, chained in a corral. Victorio, Nana, and Loco were not confined.

San Carlos was considered to be "the worst place in all Apacheria." (Ball 1970:5) The Apaches were quartered at old Camp Goodwin, which had been abandoned by the cavalry because of many deaths from malaria. Summer temperatures allegedly got as high as 140°. "There was no game, no food except the occasional meager and unfit stuff issued to them (by the Indian agent). The insects swarmed about them and almost devoured the babies." (Ball 1970:50)

During the summer, Victorio saw his people suffer and die. Finally, joined by Nana and Loco, plans for flight were carefully arranged; they evaded the cavalry for weeks, but were eventually captured and imprisoned. The Army fed them until November, 1877, and then returned them to Warm Springs. (Ball 1970:52)

Then came the insidious orders of Carleton—the orders of a man determined to exterminate the Apaches. Victorio was to take his people to San Carlos again ... that horrible place! If they did not go, the orders stated, every man, woman, or child, found off the reservation was to be shot without being given a chance to surrender.

Nana, who was considered to be the "fiercest and most implacable of all Apaches," (Ball 1970:71) and his followers had no intention of returning to San Carlos. They could have joined Juh in Mexico, but it was decided that the most feasible thing at the time was to join the Mescalero, from whom permission was obtained. In December, 1878, Nana took his Warm Springs band to Blazer's Mill on the Tularosa River in south-central New Mexico, then the headquarters of the Mescalero Apache reservation. Sixty-three were there enrolled, received ration cards, and were issued rations. They were allowed to settle in the remote and rather inaccessible Rinconada canyon—where Nana had previously (and secretly) sent most of his young men and horses. Brush arbors were built and covered with hides; wood, water, and game were abundant. (Ball 1970:25-27)

Victorio, too, came to the Rinconada encampment—with a bounty on his head—for a warrant had been issued for his arrest.

The arrival of soldiers at Blazer's caused him and his men to make their way to their sacred mountain in the San Andres, where they could not be captured.

Loco started to take his band to San Carlos on the Gila River. At the east end of Cook's Peak (north of Deming, New Mexico), they were attacked by U.S. Cavalry and several Apache were killed before Loco could convince them that they were going to San Carlos voluntarily. When the soldiers were convinced, they escorted the Apache band toward the Gila. A snowstorm forced them to turn north to Fort Apache, and Loco's group was taken to Camp Goodwin. Victorio learned of these developments, and was prepared to aid Loco, should he decide to flee to Mexico.

Nana decided to lead his people to Chihuahua by way of the Big Bend country in Texas; several other small bands joined in the dangerous journey. Victorio dashed from place to place, drawing the cavalry away from the traveling ones. It is said that Victorio took about four hundred people with him, seventy-five of them warriors; some were Mescalero and Lipan. (Ball 1970:75) In 1880, they headed north again.

Gerónimo made peace with General George Crook in 1882, but this lasted only three years. Then the Apache were forced to assemble again, and raiding was resumed. In 1886, Gerónimo brought his people forth to surrender. As a result, he was imprisoned and sent to confinement in Florida, where the Chiricahua and all associated bands were transferred.

Later, a home for them was sought in Alabama; finally, they were taken to Fort Sill, Oklahoma, "to round out a term of twenty-seven years as prisoners of war. In 1913, they were released and given the choice of taking up residence on the Mescalero Indian Reservation in New Mexico (northeast of Alamogordo) or of accepting allotments of land in Oklahoma." (*See* Opler 1942:viii) Some one hundred took the allotments, but the majority of the Chiricahua joined the Mescalero. Henceforth, the development of these groups may best be considered as the Mescalero-Chiricahua; however, scholars have been able to gain specific data from Mescalero, Chiricahua, and related informants, and thus to establish their respective past history to some degree.

In their social organization, an extensive bilateral reckoning of kinship is found among the Apache. (*See* Goodwin 1942) The Mescalero, for instance, did not require band exogamy, but marriages between kinsmen were forbidden; consequently, unions outside the band were most common. Marriages tended to be easily broken, especially during the early years of a union. Polygamy was allowed, but was rarely practiced. More usual was "serial monogamy," wherein "a married man might go to another area, perhaps on a raid, extend his residence there, and eventually marry again. The social network of an individual Mescalero was both extensive and flexible, permitting him to activate ties with a wide range of cognates and to initiate new affinal bonds to meet the demands of a specific situation." (Basehart 1967:284) Marriages with outsiders were frowned upon by the Mescalero—particularly when they resulted in the loss of a Mescalero to another group.

The ordinary house type of the Chiricahua was the dome-shaped wickiup of brush. Mother-in-law avoidance was followed, as with the Navaho. Like the Navaho, too, the Chiricahua regarded birds, insects, and coyotes as once having been people; mankind, then, is but following in the footsteps of those who have gone before. No one account of the creation of human beings seems to have existed. (*See* Opler 1942:1) Mythical personages are closely related to those of the Navaho; they bear similar names, but they have differing positions of importance in some instances.

If death were to occur in a dwelling, it was deserted; the name of the deceased was not spoken. Other death customs included hair cutting and wailing. If a funeral party were seen or a newly bereaved family encountered, a Chiricahua would avoid a meeting or join in the wailing for the dead. A successful war expedition was always followed by a victory dance.

The area east of Tularosa on U.S. Highway 70, became the Mescalero reservation, and today it covers some 460,000 acres. There the Apache have adjusted themselves to the life of their fellow Americans by becoming farmers, ranchers, loggers, machine operators, nurses, ministers, artists, carpenters, clerks, accountants, policemen, and firefighters. They were the first to offer the U.S. Forest Service a trained and organized unit of firefighters to help put down forest fires in the Southwest.

Currently, attire is much like that of any western citizen. Most of the Apache men have adopted "western wear" for everyday: colorful shirts, denim pants, cowboy boots or shoes, and fitting accessories. Most Apache men have their hair cut, and they commonly shave. Some of the Apache women still wear a one-piece dress of Mother Hubbard style, or a loose hip-length blouse overhanging full skirt. Now, the tendency with the young is to wear non-Indian clothing. Moccasins are seldom worn except at ceremonial events. The Mescalero dye their deerskin moccasins a yellow color; these are made with the peculiar up-turned toe and circular element which serves as protection against cactus spines and other prickly vegetation.

The Mescalero operate several profitable industries, including a store and Summit enterprise, a woodyard and Christmas tree market, the Ruidoso recreation area with fishing and skiing developments; they practice soil conservation and engage in cattle raising. They have an incorporated Cattle Growers Association with a manager under contract. A board of directors elected annually controls the operations. Not all members of the tribe are stock-holders in the corporation, but all stockholders are tribal members. Over 4,500 head of cattle are run on more than seven hundred sections of the reservation. An annual tour-type sale attracts buyers to the Mescalero auction from far and near. In 1969, some $300,000 worth of cattle were disposed of in less than an hour. A herd of good horses, with forty-five breeding mares, is also maintained.

The bulk of the Mescalero income is derived from timber sales and is deposited with the United States Treasury. Individual income is realized from cattle and wages, and a limited amount from small farm assignments which are made by the governing officers.

A federal charter declares the Mescalero a federal corporation. They operate under a constitution and by-laws, governed by the Mescalero Tribal Business Committee. Officers of the tribe are a president, vice-president, treasurer, and secretary; the council is composed of these and other members—numbering eleven in all—elected by eligible voters of the tribe; women may, and do, hold office as well as men. All positions and operations are supported by the tribe. They have criminal and civil codes and police themselves, as well as administer their self-government.

In recent years, the Mescalero have shown a steady increase. Reduced to 630 in 1915, they numbered about 1,740 as of 1 January 1970. This figure includes the Mescalero, those of Chiricahua ancestry, and remnants of the Lipan and other bands.

THE JICARILLA   During their early days in the Southwest, two divisions of the Jicarilla Apache were recognized. The *Hoyero* (also spelled *Ollero*), or "mountain people," and the *Llanero*, or "plains people." (*See* Harrington 1940:511) At that time, they ranged from the Chama valley eastward across what is now central and eastern Colorado into western Oklahoma, and at least as far south as present day Estancia, New Mexico. In their easternmost contacts, the Jicarilla took over certain elements of Plains Indian culture, as did the Mescalero who roamed the eastern plains.

Among the features adopted was the style of moccasins and leggings worn by the Jicarilla; natural deerskin of the moccasins was whitened, rather than dyed yellow, and the toe was without the protective up-turned feature of other Apache groups. Soles were of rawhide or cowhide. The hip-length leggings, suspended from a belt, were distinct from those worn by other Apaches. They were made from a single piece of dressed deerskin, hair side out, with the addition of a cuff, fringe, and tabs—which may represent survival of the large cuff tabs in style on the northern plains one hundred to one hundred and fifty years ago. The bottom of the cuff was cut into four tabs, each with very short self-fringe, while the cuff top had fringe about two and a half inches long. The entire legging was colored with yellow ochre, and decorative stripes commonly were added in other colors; red and green were favored. Then, a band of beading was worked on the skin with simple design units, a row of beading across the cuff being characteristic.

The men parted their hair in the middle, plaited it into two braids, which were wound with strips of deerskin and worn in front over the shoulders. At one time, they wore bangs across the forehead on a line with the cheek bones and tied their hair in a knot at the back of the head, like the Navaho and most of the Pueblo men. The favored ornaments worn by the men were large earrings of the old Navaho type—a silver circlet with a loose silver bead dangling at its lower circumference. They also wore short bead pendants suspended from the pierced earlobe. A kerchief was commonly tied about the neck, with ends falling on the chest, "cowboy fashion."

Deerskin garments of Plains type were worn by the Jicarilla women; they never adopted the Mother Hubbard style of dress taken over by other Apache women.

The Jicarilla Apache were a problem to the white men during the mid-1850's, (See Taylor 1970) and were among those pacified by Kit Carson in 1868. Following this event, they were first placed on the Mescalero reservation, and then in an area just to the east of the Navaho—putting them, it would seem, in or near the territory that had been occupied by their ancestors. In each instance, such hard fighting between the Jicarilla and other Indians resulted that they had to be moved again.

The north half of the present Jicarilla reservation was established in 1887; the south half was added in 1908; together, they include nearly three-quarters of a million acres of varied plain, semidesert, mountain and forest land dotted with small lakes. These holdings extend south from the Colorado border for approximately sixty-five miles to the vicinity of Cuba on N.M. Highway S-44. Altitude varies from 6,400 to 8,200 feet above sea level. The agency headquarters is at Dulce on Highway S-17, some twenty-seven miles west of Chama.

Within the last few years, the Jicarilla have improved their water and sewer systems; they have built many modern homes on the reservation and have remodeled old ones; a church has been erected. Several families live in new trailers. Many new miles of paved roads lead to and traverse the Jicarilla holdings. As of 1 January 1970, the census recognized 1,742 tribal members—a growth of 1,157 since an epidemic of influenza reduced them to 585 just fifty years ago.

Apache men are good stockmen. The Jicarilla own some 20,000 head of sheep, around 1,500 cattle, and, too, many horses. Lamb and wool sales net significant income annually; cattle produce less revenue. Hundreds of gas wells have been drilled on the reservation, and more than one hundred producing oil wells. Royalties from these wells make up an important part of the Jicarilla income. New industries that will employ people dwelling there are being attracted to the reservation. Raw materials and products of agriculture, livestock, and forestry, all-year recreation activities, great power potential, and favorable market conditions are among the inducements at hand.

New Mexico has figured importantly in movie making the last few years, largely through undertakings of state agencies. Now, the Jicarilla have provided a good example of Apache acumen. On their own behalf, the initiative was taken to promote commercial motion pictures. Making contact with the Harvest Productions of Los Angeles, the Jicarilla agreed to finance the movie, *A Gunfight*, up to $2 million. Portions of the film were shot near Santa Fe, interior scenes were made in Hollywood, and other portions, including a bullfight, were made on location near Ocuna, Spain.

One of the Jicarilla men, who had been tribal accountant for nearly twenty years, resigned to become program affairs director for the BIA's Jicarilla agency. He and another of his tribesmen, the agency superintendent, went to Spain to help coordinate European sales of the film. They, incidentally, financed the trip from personal funds. European salesmen had already offered $1,750,000 for the movie. The first $2 million of profits is designated for the Jicarilla tribe (but as this book goes to press, only a few thousand dollars had been received, and interest losses were mounting). (Sandoval 1971)

The picture, released in the spring of 1971, featured such stars as Kirk Douglas and Johnny Cash, and an Italian actor, Raf Vallone, for the bullfight scene.

Another Jicarilla accomplishment of note is the construction of an Olympic-size, heated indoor swimming pool and recreation area at Dulce. It was jointly funded by HUD and the tribe, the cost of $1.5 million being met on a fifty-fifty basis. With this underway, many of the Jicarilla—adults and children alike—began learning to swim. Arrangements were made with personnel of a camp on the Brazos River, near Chama, for two groups of twenty-one each to take four weeks of instruction. Tribal officials were included; some prepared themselves for lifesaving and instructor's certificates. The facility was dedicated on 7 January 1972.

The Jicarilla govern by means of an eight-member council of male and female members who stand for election every two years, in accordance with an adopted constitution and by-laws. A president, vice-president, secretary, business manager, director of the tribe's Game and Fish Department, and an executive committee are chosen by the council. According to the constitution, only business surplus can be distributed on a dividend basis, as with any other corporation. Funds of their corporation have been allocated for training of personnel and the construction of facilities to assist firms providing the greatest economic benefit to the Jicarilla.

More than two hundred Jicarilla derive individual income from tribal employment; over fifty have positions with the BIA and a few with the U.S. Public Health Service; others have miscellaneous sources of revenue. Education in general receives major attention, and up-to-date school facilities are provided. In 1956, the Jicarilla tribe placed one million dollars in an Albuquerque bank to finance education for children and adults who want to learn new jobs, and to aid worthy students who do not have sufficient money of their own.

As a result of having shown such sound operation of their 742,303 acres of land, permitting balanced programs in range use, outdoor recreation, and game management, the Jicarilla were honored, in the spring of 1970, by a Department of the Interior Conservation Service Award—that department's top honor. In a letter to the president of the Jicarilla council, the Secretary of the Interior offered "recognition of the significant progress of the (tribe) not only in conservation and improvements of their natural resources, but also in the variety and intensity of the management of their own affairs, and their cooperation and involvement with other federal and state agencies." (Anonymous 1970c)

THE WESTERN APACHES The major Western Apache divisions embrace the White Mountain, Cibecue, San Carlos, and northern and southern Tonto groups that now dwell in southeastern Arizona. Although each division has certain distinctions, such as linguistic dialects and religious and social practices, they share basic characteristics. Their terrain is cut by high mountain barriers which rise to well over 11,000 feet, from lowland areas of some 2,600 feet elevation. These natural barriers tended to isolate one band from another, so that each came to have fairly well-defined territories. No political affiliations existed between the various groups, in the past or at present. They were relatively peaceful until forced to develop a raiding pattern by foreign peoples, Indian and non-Indian. As with other Indian peoples, treaties were made and broken.

The family constitutes the Apache economic unit. This includes the normal pattern of those adhering to a matrilineal system, where children are born into the clan of the mother: grandparents, married daughters and their husbands, unmarried sons, and children of the daughters. Each family is bound together by certain rights and duties. The clan system—which still operates to a degree—cuts across groups and bands. Marriage within one's clan is forbidden. In the Apache clans, cousins are called "brother" and "sister." Marriage between cousins is taboo. Families live in relatively large groups with the home of the mother being the family center. Mothers and daughters are very close and they carry on many tasks together. When a son marries, his obligations henceforth are to the family of his mother-in-law; he is to protect and work for the domestic circle into which he marries. If a man's wife dies, he may remarry. Frequently, he marries a sister of his deceased wife. Marriages now are in accordance with the white man's practices.

In their chosen locale, livelihood did not come easily. Primary foodstuffs consisted of wild game and fruits, seeds and nuts of indigenous plants; some corn, beans, and squash were raised. Conflicts grew through the years, culminating in a terrific battle between the Anglo-Americans and the Apache in 1862. Mangas Coloradas, a Nednhi Apache, had come to the fore, and was then an elderly man; he was wounded in battle, but recovered. He was ready for peace and, being tricked by a promising overture, he went to an army camp in New Mexico where he was murdered in January, 1863. His son, Mangus, became leader. An intensive and treacherous campaign against the Apache was waged by the army and by civilians. Scores of Apache were killed, but Victorio and other leaders retaliated. It is said that the U.S. government spent some $38 million from 1862 to 1871 in its effort to exterminate the Apaches.

General Crook, who knew the Indians well, then was assigned the task of "taming" all of the Apache bands in Arizona. A few swift campaigns resulted in subduing the Western Apache and the Yavapai, with whom extensive intermarriage had taken place. They were placed on reservations at San Carlos and at Fort Apache. Crook hired Apache men as scouts, and programs in agriculture and livestock raising were initiated. Uneasy peace reigned for several years; no consistent Indian policy was followed. As related above, at one time the Chiricahua were forced to dwell among the Western Apache, as were the Tonto and some of the Yavapai. Of course, this was unsuccessful. In large part, Apache scouts led to the downfall of the Apaches—for they knew the haunts and practices of their people, and how to lead the soldiers to them.

Through all the tumultuous decades, the Chiricahua and associated bands were hardest hit by their foes. On the other hand, the Western Apache fared much better. It is said that they had a population of about 4,000 in the 1860's and that in 1890 their census enumerated 4,138, and they still occupied their homeland, an area reaching from Flagstaff and Showlow to the Santa Catalina, Rincon, and Whetstone Mountains on the south, and from the Camp Verde-Superior alignment on the west almost to the New Mexico border on the east. (*See* Baldwin 1965:52)

In November, 1871, the original White Mountain reservation was established; it included the present Fort Apache and San Carlos reservations. In 1897, the area was divided and separated into the Fort Apache and the San Carlos reservations, respectively.

Over the years, their acreage was continually reduced by white men who hungered for the valuable resources of the Apaches—minerals and grazing lands especially. By 1920, leases held by whites amounted to approximately five-eights of the San Carlos reservation, and the lands were being destroyed by illegal grazing of thousands of unregistered cattle. The San Carlos lands were not allotted, and it is said that "due to the peculiar topographical conditions of the reservation with its small patches of ground suitable for farming and its scattered watering places in the grazing areas, individual allotments would never be practical." (Arizona Writers' Project 1941:33)

Agents interested in the Apache welfare came on the scene by 1923, and the overgrazing situation began to change. Leases were gradually terminated and the lands returned to the Indians (the last outside grazing leases ran out in 1948). (Anonymous 1969d) Indian organization, or participation in Apache interests was started in 1924 with development of the resources of tribal and individual potentialities, "which consisted of cattle interests, small gardens, and a home security or social system." (Arizona Writers' Project 1941:33) Until 1932, these efforts were carried on by community meetings. Then, a Business Council was organized. Its plans were sound, with result that progress was constant. A self-supporting program was inaugurated and meetings held by various groups; grazing fees per head of all cattle sold were established, permitting the San Carlos to build up and maintain one of the largest cattle ownerships as a self-supporting economic venture, without required assistance from tribal or federal funds.

The Apache ability to understand the fundamentals of self-government by actual practice led to almost unanimous acceptance of the Reorganization Act of 1934 and a favorable vote on their constitution; the latter provides for the election by the Apache of a tribal council as the governing body. "This was followed by acceptance, with some amendments as applying particularly to this tribe (San Carlos, White Mountain), of the Law and Order Regulation as approved by the Secretary of the Interior November 27, 1935, and the immediate functioning of the reservation under these new regulations. The Indian Court, working with the Indian Council, claims they had been using practically these same regulations for several years, which resulted in little or no confusion in the change-over to an approved and regulated method of court procedure." And the San Carlos took over "the responsibility and duties of this splendid piece of legislation with little change in their economic or social standards and procedure," (Arizona Writers' Project 1941-34) with gratifying results. Law infractions are handled by native judges, with court order kept by native police. Court procedure is similar to the white man's.

Other programs administered include general administration,

construction and maintenance of roads, employment assistance, forestry and range conservation, soil and moisture conservation, irrigation, plant management, education, and welfare.

Agency headquarters of the 1,648,000-acre reservation located in Gila, Graham, and Pinal counties of Arizona is at San Carlos, southeast of Globe. Apache living on the reservation number about 5,000. Their sources of livelihood come primarily from livestock, mining, and timber activities. The tribe operates general stores at San Carlos and at Bylas, on U.S. Highway 70; and a few privately owned businesses are permitted on the reservation. A number of the San Carlos are employed at the copper mines in Globe, Miami, and Superior. Some work on a seasonal basis for highway contractors on road construction projects; others are employed by the BIA in various capacities on the reservation. Out-of-door recreation facilities have been developed, offering hunting, fishing, camping, horseback riding, etc.

A combined BIA-public school for grades one through four is in operation at the agency headquarters. From the fifth grade up, San Carlos children attend the Globe Public Schools and the fully accredited Globe High School. A Catholic elementary school in San Carlos takes children through the second grade.

Unfortunately, recent years have seen adverse changes occurring among the San Carlos people. During 1973, Joel Nilsson, a general assignment reporter for the *Arizona Daily Star*, lived for a month on their reservation and looked at all facets of San Carlos life. He found unemployment responsible for many ills. This fluctuated between 25 and 40 per cent. Almost two thousand of the Indians were on one kind of welfare or another; over 900 of some 1,000-odd reservation homes were determined unfit to live in; about 20 per cent of the Indian population had alcoholism problems, and the rate of suicide was rising. Although Apache law states that students must stay in school until the age of eighteen or until they have completed high school, about seventy youngsters in the sixteen-eighteen bracket were not attending school.

A struggle for leadership within the San Carlos group and questionable fiscal practices caused serious conflicts and added to the difficulties. (Anonymous 1973)

The White Mountain Apache live on the Fort Apache Indian reservation in Navajo, Apache, and Gila counties of Arizona. This adjoins the San Carlos reservation and comprises an area of some seventy-five miles east-west and forty-five miles north-south, with an acreage of 1,656,698, or 2,601 square miles. Holbrook lies eighty-five miles north of the reservation headquarters, which is at Whiteriver, about four miles north of Fort Apache (site of a former military post). From the semiarid southwest corner of the reservation, where the elevation is about 2,700 feet, the terrain ranges upward to 11,459 feet at the northeast (Mount Thomas). Nearly half of the population lives in permanent cabins or modern homes; others occupy wickiups which are generally modified somewhat from the original structure pattern—a small entrance hall with door is common. Clan ties are maintained.

Like the San Carlos, the White Mountain Apache operate as a tribe under provisions of the Reorganization Act of 1934; they have a constitution. The council consists of a chairman and vice-chairman who are elected by popular vote for four-year terms; and nine members, two of whom are elected by popular vote of the Cibecue, Oak Creek, and Grasshopper districts, two similarly by the Carrizo, Forestdale, and Cedar Creek districts, and two by the East Fork, Turkey Creek, and Seven Mile districts, and three members by the Canyon Day and Whiteriver North Fork districts. Excepting the latter district, these are elected for terms of two and four years; those receiving the most votes serve for the longer period, and the others for the two-year term; the exception elects two members at alternating elections for four-year terms. The council has authority to appropriate tribal funds for the welfare and benefit of the tribe and for the development and protection of the reservation and its resources—with the approval of the Department of the Interior.

The White Mountain Apache entered into the cattle business to a limited extent, about 1900 with the introduction of cattle from Mexico. In 1917, some 800 head of grade Herefords were brought from Mexico to Fort Apache. From this beginning, the White Mountain Tribal Herd was increased by the purchase from time to time of cows and bulls, and the present herd of fine stock numbering 2,200 head was developed. Issues were made to individual Indians. This enterprise operates a tribally-owned ranch of nearly 138,000 acres on the southeast corner of the reservation.

Individual livestock owners are organized into eight livestock associations for management and sales, but all cattle are individually owned and branded. A stockman is chosen for each district to perform the duties of the old-time foreman; each district has a three-man board of directors. A manager is in charge of the tribally-owned cattle, and a general livestock manager looks after the individual members' stock, which number 15,000 Herefords.

This is one of the most competitive cattle spreads in the American West. The cattle industry alone puts between $30,000 and $40,000 back into the tribal coffers annually.

Various other enterprises are operated, each with a managing board of directors; one is the Fort Apache Timber Company which employs some one hundred and ten members of the tribe; this produces an annual income exceeding $3,000,000. Another undertaking, the White Mountain Apache Enterprises, consists of summer homesite leases, five stores and service stations, several boat dock concessions with boat rental, first class tourist facilities, a liquor store in McNary, and the Apache Flame. The White Mountain Recreation Enterprise, which includes the largest privately owned recreation area in the West (with several lakes and 300 miles of trout streams), controls game management, fishing and hunting licenses, campgrounds, and game wardens.

The White Mountain Apache, like the Jicarilla, were cited by the Secretary of the Interior in April, 1970. Their citation was in recognition of an "outstanding conservation program"—this being for the "preservation of the Arizona (Apache) trout, which had faced extinction until the Apaches began their preservation work in 1952." (Anonymous 1970c) Efforts of the White Mountain Apache increased the number of trout and prevented further hybridization.

These Apache are also engaged in an intensive program to provide housing, training, education, and employment opportunities for their 5,300 members. Approximately 2,500 members are now attending school from Head Start through universities. School attendance of children between the ages of six and eighteen is enforced by the council. In 1956, a scholarship program was initiated for the aid of tribal members interested in continuing their education beyond high school. The majority of students are in public schools, nearly one-fourth attend BIA schools on the reservation, and about one-fourth are in mission schools. An outstanding summer youth program is carried on each year.

Health facilities are provided by the U.S. Public Health Service, with a hospital in Whiteriver and clinics in the various communities.

Law and order is maintained by a Special Officer and a force of ten policemen. All offenses are handled by the Tribal Court, with exception of the ten major crimes which, as among the other Southwestern Indian groups, go to the Federal Court. (Young

1961:284)* Tribal police have the same official status as officers in any other community, and they cooperate fully with county, state, and federal law enforcement agencies. The Tribal Court was established in 1940; it consists of one Chief Judge and two Associate Judges. Cases coming within the jurisdiction of the court are heard daily and, where evidence is sufficient to convict, penalties are assessed according to the Law and Order Code.

RELIGIOUS BELIEFS AND CEREMONIES

The Apache awareness of deity and their attitude toward a supreme being have been little understood, and less promulgated.

In general, the Apache recognize a supreme deity of impersonal character to whom no sex is attributed, but who is thought of as the creator—a deity that may be identified as *Yusn*, as *Ussen*, or Giver-of-life. This omnipotent one is the source of all supernatural power and is "the maker of world and man," but since the creation, little direct contact has prevailed between Giver-of-life and man.

However, supernatural power reaches mankind and exercises strong control over worldly affairs. In contrast to this, it is noted that the "Giver-of-life is remote and nebulous to the Apache mind. . . . The power of Giver-of-life becomes translated into specific ceremonies. It is these ceremonies which warmly and intimately impinge against Apache life . . . and dominate Apache religious thinking. Giver-of-life may be mentioned in the opening prayer of a rite. Thereafter, however, the attention shifts to the specific power whose aid the ceremony is attempting to win." (Opler 1935:66[†])

At every point in life, the Apache seeks supernatural aid in meeting his problems and conducting his affairs. These aids from the supernaturals are manifest as ceremonies that are markedly similar in pattern, though they differ widely in detail. Nearly all of them are initiated with ceremonial smoking, then throwing of pollen to the four directions, prayer, and singing.

The Apache, we are told, think of power

as a mighty force that pervades the universe. Some of it filters through to the hands of man. But to become manifest to man, power must approach him through the medium of certain agencies and channels, must "work through" something. The most conspicuous of these agencies are certain natural

---

*These include murder, manslaughter, rape, assault with intent to kill, arson, burglary, larceny, robbery, incest, and assault with a deadly weapon. An eleventh crime is embezzlement of tribal funds.

[†]Opler (1941:281) says *Yusn* [Ussen] is from the Spanish *díos*—thus a Christian transfer of deific name.

phenomena such as the lightning or sun, and a number of animals, principally the bear, snake, owl, and coyote . . . but there are scores of possibilities. (Opler 1935:66*)

An Apache may accept or reject the power offered to him. Every Apache man or woman is a potential recipient of supernatural power. If the power is accepted, the recipient, it is said, " . . . is given directions for conducting a ceremony; he is instructed in the songs, the prayers, the four ceremonial gifts he must ask in return for his services, and the taboos, if any, which he must observe himself and impose on the one for whom he is working." (Opler 1935:67-68) One may be given as many as five different ceremonies. Thus, it is "that an Apache becomes 'loaded up with powers.'" A man's power is not public property. (Opler 1935:68; *cf.* Ball 1970:11) Often, no one other than a person's own family may know of his ceremony. Ceremonies may be transmitted from one person to another, as from elder to younger people. When a ceremony is taught to someone outside the family circle, a fee is always charged by the teacher.

As do the Navaho, the Apache account for death, disease, and disaster as power manipulated by malevolent persons, or power itself seeking to do harm. Appropriate terms are applied to such agencies, as for beneficial supernatural powers.

The ceremonials of the Apache have not had the same publicity as have those of the Navaho. But ceremonies are performed as cures, to set things right, or to ward off possible evil. The majority of Apache ceremonies are curative rites which are carried out by shamans who have obtained supernatural power from a great number of sources, chiefly from the potent Mountain Spirits, supernatural beings called *Gáhan* or *Gáhe*. All Apaches consider the ceremonial circuit as clockwise; and few are the things not connected with the number four.

Once a shaman has been engaged to conduct a ceremony to cure an ill person, the procedure is to dress and paint the bodies of several men—usually four—to represent the Mountain Spirits. These dance into view, approaching the patient, or the camps from which the illness is to be exorcised; and by dancing, giving forth distinctive calls, and making gestures, the objective is attained. Songs are sung by the shaman while the dancers are being prepared and while they are performing. The songs function as messages to the supernaturals and acquaint them with an aid required by the shaman.

*All quotations from Opler 1935 are reproduced by permission of the American Anthropological Association from *American Anthropologist,* Vol. 37, No. 1 (1935).

The Mountain Spirits are considered to be numerous and they inhabit many mountains. Like all supernaturals and ritual objects, they are associated with colors and directions. Therefore, the Mountain Spirits of each cardinal direction are represented by a leader, and a particular color is attributed to him. Although the associations vary somewhat, the most common color representations are said to be:

> Black Mountain Spirit is the leader of a single file
> from the east;
> Blue Mountain Spirit is the leader of a single file
> from the south;
> Yellow Mountain Spirit is the leader of a single file
> from the west; and
> White (or Grey) Mountain Spirit is the leader of a
> single file from the north.

The blue, or turquois, color and the cross are used extensively in ceremonial symbolism. Pollen represents growth and vitality. (*See* Opler 1938a:154-155) Abalone is considered as pollen also—perhaps "water pollen."

Studies have revealed that not such a wide gulf exists between the Navaho and Apache basic cultures as was once thought. As might be expected, the major Jicarilla cycle of mythology closely parallels the Navaho. For instance, the Jicarilla puberty ceremony is similar to that of the Navaho. It is not tribal, but is held by a girl's family or clan when she is ready for marriage.

The Jicarilla observe a bear dance upon call of a curer, or shaman. The name is taken from a Ute Indian ceremony which has nothing to do with bears. In fact it is a Holiness rite (*See* Opler 1938b:27-44), performed within a brush corral, as is the Navaho Mountain Topway. Small fires are lit around the interior of the enclosure. A medicine tipi is erected at the west end. Where the Navaho would drum on a basket to set the rhythm, several Jicarilla men rub notched sticks together, resting the end of a rasp on a basket. This appears to be an element derived from the Ute. It produces a resonant, powerful sound which is very effective. While the main ceremony—the most sacred part, in which dry paintings (sandpaintings) are made—goes on in the lodge, women select partners and dance with them outside, somewhat after the manner of a Navaho squaw dance, except that no payment is made; one steps out when he tires of dancing. A dramatic entrance occurs when a group of masked dancers accompanied by sacred clowns comes onto the scene. Certain cautions have been advised by people who have attended the bear dance; it is suggested that visitors should not attempt to witness the ceremony unless they know the Jicarilla well, and have adequate information regarding situations that might arise.

On 4 July, the Jicarilla hold a feast, without attendant ceremonies. Annually, a two-day celebration is held on 14 and 15 September, near Horse Lake. This reenacts the yearly reunion of the two divisions of the tribe—the mountain people and those of the plains. On the fifteenth, they perform an imitation of the ceremonial race that is run at Taos during the San Gerónimo fiesta. At night, a round dance is held. The friendship between the Jicarilla and Taos Indians is so close that each attends the other's feast, or *fiesta*, in large numbers; Taos people participate in the Jicarilla race, and a few of the Apache take some part in the ceremony at Taos.

Unlike other Southwestern Athabascan peoples, the Mescalero do not tell an emergence legend in the course of which reference is made to the creation and to the origins of the major ceremonials. Instead, they have utilized the *coyote cycle* to introduce these elements. This cycle is a connected series of episodes that describe the travels and adventures of a trickster, the attributes and characteristics of which are sometimes human, and again, those of an animal. Coyote is a type character that reveals a remarkable self-portrait of the Apache—a shrewd and powerful satire of his culture and of human foibles. (Opler 1938a:214)

The Apache have a common custom of referring to something else than that which is mentioned, to something which resembles it, as for example, calling an owl's ears a "hat"—much to the merriment of all. In speech, direct reference is not made to a bear; to do so would "run the risk of seeing the bear shortly afterwards and of catching the sickness (a painful disease that might be contracted)." (Opler 1938a:217)* To throw food about or to handle it carelessly is thought by the Apache to be very dangerous and unlucky. Bones are not thrown around; they are placed in a neat pile and disposed of at once. To do otherwise "is to invite the loss of hunting skill and shortage of food." (Opler 1938a:217)

With the Mescalero, the girls' puberty ceremony is their most important public observance; and this was true of the Chiricahua. (*See* Opler 1938a:143-151) Two ceremonies are held for girls who go through the performance. Much symbolism is worked into the rites.

At that time, Sun and Earth are important agencies. First, a large brush tipi is erected, representing the universe. It is said to be constructed of "old age staffs and gray hair"—to give long life to the girls for whom the ceremony is held. A girl being inducted to womanhood represents White Painted Woman, the Apache priestess who officiates with the Sun's representative; she is the model for all Apache womankind. The rites of induction, throughout, symbolize the recreation of White Painted Woman (comparable to Changing Woman of the Navaho). At the end of the rites, the tipi is taken down. All is in charge of the "medicine man," or shaman. Second is the sun greeting ceremony. This takes place early in the morning of the first day of the observances, and again early in the morning of the final day.

MESCALERO APACHE SONG OF THE GOTAL CEREMONY

The black turkey gobbler, under the east, the middle
of his trail; toward us it is about to dawn.
The black turkey gobbler, the tips of his beautiful tail;
above us the dawn whitens.
The black turkey gobbler, the tips of his beautiful tail;
above us the dawn becomes yellow.
The sunbeams stream forward, dawn boys, with
shimmering shoes [sandals] of yellow.
On top of the sunbeams that stream toward us they
are dancing.
At the east the rainbow moves forward, dawn maidens,
with shimmering shoes and shirts of yellow
dance over us.
Beautifully over us it is dawning.
Above us among the mountains the herbs are
becoming green.
Above us on the top of the mountains the herbs are
becoming yellow.
Above us among the mountains, with shoes of yellow
I go around the fruits and the herbs that shimmer.
Above us among the mountains, the shimmering fruits
with shoes and shirts of yellow are bent toward him.
On the beautiful mountains above it is daylight.

From: *Gotal: A Mescalero Apache Ceremony*, by P. E. Goddard (1909:216)—an adolescence rite for girls.

At night, the Gáhan—those supernatural beings who live in the mountain caves and beneath the horizon in the cardinal directions—

appear as masked dancers. For each four dancers, a shaman is present to dress and decorate them. He performs a ceremony while they are being painted and attired. The painting of the upper portions of the body is accompanied by a song, and the mask and headdress are held toward the four cardinal directions before they are worn. The dancers must be painted differently for each of the four nights of the ceremony. These dancers approach a large bonfire, around which they dance. They come in single file from each of the four directions. They come four times, swaying and uttering a peculiar call. Each carries painted wands which are brandished vigorously.

The headdresses are spectacular. They are made of thin strips of wood, arranged in various patterns: crosses, fans, circles, and so on. They are colorfully decorated and further embellished with tin ornaments and downy plumes. The upper, ornamented part of the headdress is supported on a length of small sapling bent to fit around the head. This is covered with black cloth which falls over the dancer's head and is gathered in to cover it closely. Tiny eyeholes are cut in the front. Above these, shiny buttons or brass paper fasteners or metal discs are attached, which give the mask a fantastic appearance in the firelight. This striking headdress has led to incorrect designations of the dance. It is spoken of as a "devil dance," or "crown dance," whereas it is actually the mountain spirits dance. Since these mountain spirits, or Gáhan, are helpful beings who introduced the dance to the Apache as a curing ceremony, one sees how serious a misnomer is this. Portions of this dance are often presented at public celebrations, such as pow-wows, the Nizhoni Dances in Albuquerque, programs at the Institute of American Indian Arts in Santa Fe, and the like—where they are received with great enthusiasm.

Among the Gáhan personators is one called the Grey One, who may take the place of White Mountain Spirit. He is a clown who caricatures the movements of the other dancers; he goes through all sorts of capers, amuses the public in general, and serves as messenger. This character compares with Born-of-water of the Navaho. While the Gáhan dance, rites are conducted in the big tipi by the shaman, the girls participating, and the women attending them. On the fourth night, the girls dance throughout the night. At first daylight, they leave the tipi for a rest period, returning at sunrise.

Finally, the girls take part in a footrace, running to the east around a basket filled with ceremonial paraphernalia and back to where deerskins have been laid out on the ground in front of the tipi. The shaman and his assistants sing four chants and during each chant the girls run. Each time, the basket is moved nearer to the deerskins. During the last chant, the girls stop at the basket and each takes a feather from it. They then circle round the basket and run far to the east. When they return, they enter their own tipi. During these races, the ceremonial tipi is dismantled. Then, gifts are thrown to the spectators and the ceremony ends. The girls, however, must remain near their tipi for four days and nights. They must observe certain taboos. After this period, they return to everyday life. (*See* Ball 1970:37-43, 207n2); (*see also* Breuninger 1970)

After this ceremony, the girls, theoretically, are ready for marriage. Traditionally, the shaman will give instructions to the young men whenever they present themselves and request it. For instance, a youth may bring to the shaman a gift of pierced blue stone with an eagle feather through it. Then, night after night, until the young man has learned, the rhythmic beat of drums can be heard at the shaman's wickiup. Thus, the songs and dances are perpetuated and the unrecorded ceremonials preserved. A few of the minor ceremonies last a short time only. The major ones are given over a period of from one to four days. Some have their own set of songs, others have prayers with words similar to songs. The songs and prayers must be used in proper sequence. Many ceremonies have their own paraphernalia: charms, certain plants or animal parts. These contain power and are used for drawing out sickness from a patient. Pollen is the most important ceremonial offering; white shell, turquois, jet, and catlinite are sacred and potent, and each has directional significance; eagle feathers are important in religious rites.

Curing ceremonies are usually held for one person only, but a few rites can be given in time of epidemics to ward off the disease from all. Other ceremonies for the good of the community, holy rites, may be held in the spring and summer when lightning, snakes, and other harmful agents are present.

In olden times, after a young man had chosen a girl for a wife, it was required that he get the consent of his people; then he made his desire known to the girl's parents. Generally, his father or uncle would do the honors for him, after which came the real proposal. Presents were offered to the girl and to her family. Wealth was counted chiefly in horses and dressed deerskins; in the night, the suitor would tie one or more horses near the girl's wickiup. A single animal was considered a poor offering. If the girl took the horses and fed and watered them, the indication was that the proposal had been accepted. If the animals were not cared for, the proposal was rejected.

Wedding ceremonies were observed by a feast and celebration that lasted three days. During that time, the betrothed couple seldom saw or spoke to each other. Formerly, after a marriage, the young couple built a wickiup near that of the wife's mother; today they may live with whichever family group is more convenient.

The Mescalero hold the puberty ceremony at the beginning of July, the erection of the tipi taking place on the morning of 1 July. This is the only instance in which a Mescalero ceremony is conducted on a fixed calendar date, a fact that derives from an old government order which forbade the holding of ceremonies at any other time of the year.

Among the Western Apache, the puberty ceremony for girls was one of their major observances, when the mountain spirits appeared. In addition to its ritual importance, the occasion was an important social event. Wealthy families held the full four-day ceremonial, while poorer ones had a one-day event. Today, these ceremonials continue, but they have lost much of their significance and influence. They are usually conducted during the 4 July celebration and the reservation fair of the Fort Apache in August or September. The Gáhan attire and accoutrement are similar to those of the Mescalero, but the wands that are brandished and the headdresses are decorated in such manner as to make them distinctive, one group from the other.

The Western Apache still recognize and respect their shamans, but they have very limited influence, especially on the younger generations.

CALENDAR OF ANNUAL
.... INDIAN EVENTS

NOTE: Do NOT take pictures, make sketches or recordings, or
        take notes without obtaining permission. This is
        VERY IMPORTANT!

In the pueblos are plazas, and the ranchería peoples and other
Indian groups have their dance places, where ceremonial events are
presented. Many observances occur over a period of several days,
but of these the major portions are held in the kivas or in places
where only the initiated ones may witness them. Parts that may be
seen by the public are customarily attended by adults and children,
Indian and non-Indian.

Remember that these are sacred and commemorative rituals. It
is expected that visitors will be *quiet and respectful.*

Ceremonies are held in Hopiland throughout the year. The
dates of these are determined according to Hopi customs and
traditions, without reference to the BIA personnel. Exact dates are
made known a few days in advance only, even to the Hopi. During
the summertime, one or more ceremonies or dances are held usually
each weekend.

Indian dances and ceremonies are based on Indian needs and
Indian time. To translate these to the white man's calendar is not
always practicable. It is advisable to check locally whenever
possible.

JAN 1   Taos turtle dance usually (*See* Dutton 1972a: 3-12); dances in many of the
            pueblos on New Year's and/or three succeeding days, e.g. cloud dance at San
            Juan.

JAN 3   Isleta corn, turtle, and various dances

JAN 6   King's Day: installation of secular officers; dances in most of the pueblos
            during afternoon; buffalo or deer dance at Taos, eagle dance at San Ildefonso.
            Dancing in the Keres pueblos. Dancers go to the houses of people named *Reyes*
            (kings), where dwellers are waiting on the roofs. After the dancers perform for
            a while, the house owner and family members throw gifts to the dancers below
            and the gathered crowd. Everybody scrambles for presents, but most are aimed
            directly to the dancers. The gifts include bread, canned and boxed foods, fruit,
            tobacco, soft drinks, and household items. Many pueblos have dances on the
            three succeeding days.

JAN 23   San Ildefonso feast day—animal dances in one plaza, Comanche dance in the other

JAN   (Late January) Acoma and Laguna governor's fiesta

FEB 2   San Felipe buffalo dance; also dances in several other pueblos

FEB 4–5   *Llano* dances, *Los Comanches,* at Taos (Spanish-American interpretation of Plains Indian dances)

FEB 15   Dances at San Juan; perhaps turtle dance at Taos, eagle dance at Santo Domingo

FEB   (Usually in February) Hopi *Powamû* (bean dance)—first rites of the katsina cult

FEB   (Late February) Isleta evergreen dance

MAR   (Palm Sunday) Most pueblos, green corn dances, ceremonial foot races

MAR-APR   (Easter Sunday and succeeding two or three days) Dances in most pueblos; ceremonial foot races. Several pueblos observe ditch-opening, or *acequia,* ceremonies with dances; some play ceremonial shinny.

MAR-APR   (During Holy Week, with the climax on Easter) Yaqui Indians have elaborate celebrations at Barrio Libra (south Tucson) and at Guadalupe near Phoenix. Deer dancers, *matachines, pascolas, fariseos,* et al., take part. (*See* Painter and Sayles 1962:24) On the first Friday after Easter, the Tucson Festival Society sponsors an annual pageant that commemorates the founding of Mission San Xavier del Bac. Papago and Yaqui dancers participate.

MAR   Phoenix Plains Indian Club sponsors Scottsdale All-Indian Day

MAR   Gila River Pima *Mul-chu-tha* at Sacaton, Arizona

MAR 27   Dances generally at the Keres pueblos and Jémez

MAR   (Late March) Indian Trade Fair, Pima-Maricopa and Yavapai-Apache communities, near Scottsdale, Arizona

SPRINGTIME   Colorado River tribes hold motor boat races and Northern Yuma County Fair at Parker, Arizona

APR   (Last Saturday) *Nizhoni* dances at Johnson Gymnasium, University of New Mexico, Albuquerque; numerous Indian groups in beautiful costumes (benefit)

APR or MAY   Ute Mountain Ute bear dances

MAY 1   San Felipe feast day, green corn dance (two large groups)

MAY 3   Taos ceremonial races (about 8:00-10:00 a.m.); Cochiti corn dance (Coming of the Rivermen)

MAY 14   Taos San Ysidro fiesta (blessing of fields); candle light procession May 15

MAY   (About 29 May through June 4) Tesuque corn or flag dance (blessing of fields)

MAY   (Late May) Salt River Pima Industrial Fair

MAY   (Last week of May or first week of June) Southern Ute bear dance

JUNE 6   Zuñi rain dance

JUNE 13   Sandía feast day, corn dance; observance of San Antonio's Day dances at Taos (corn dance), San Juan, Santa Clara, San Ildefonso, Cochiti, and Paguate

JUNE 20   Isleta governor's dance

JUNE 24   San Juan feast day, dancing there; observance of San Juan's Day dances at Taos (afternoon), Isleta,* Cochiti, Santa Ana, Laguna; Acoma and Jémez rooster pulls

JUNE 29   San Pedro's Day at Laguna, Acoma, Santa Ana, San Felipe, Santo Domingo, Cochiti, and Isleta—generally rooster pulls

JUNE   (Late June, or during July) Hopi *Nimán* ("going home")—last rites of the katsina cult; katsinas are believed to go to their traditional home on San Francisco Peak. One of the ceremonial officers from Shungopavi announced that the Nimán rites and snake dances are closed because "rules against recording, picture taking and hand-drawing have been disregarded again by both Hopis and non-Indians . . . and sacred prayer feathers have been taken away." (Action Line, *Albuquerque Journal,* 15 August 1972)

JULY 1-4   Mescalero Apache *Gáhan* ceremonial at Mescalero, New Mexico

JULY 4   Jicarilla Apache feast (no ceremonies); Nambé celebration at Nambé Falls—special events and dances

JULY 4   Flagstaff Pow-Wow (Check annually)

JULY 14   Cochiti, feast day of San Buenaventura—corn dance

JULY   (Mid-July or August) Ute sun dance, Ignacio, Colorado

JULY 24   Acoma rooster pull

JULY 25   Santiago's feast day at Acoma, Laguna, Cochiti, and Taos—dances, rabbit hunt

JULY 26   Feast day of Santa Ana, corn dances; also at Taos

JULY   (Late July) Santa Clara festival at Puyé cliff ruins; arts and crafts exhibits, dances (entrance fee entitles one to take photographs)

AUG 2   Jémez, old Pecos bull dance

AUG 4   Santo Domingo feast day, corn dance—large and fine; two groups

AUG 10   San Lorenzo's feast day; corn dances at Picurís, Laguna, and Acomita

AUG 12   Santa Clara feast day; corn dances

AUG 15   Zía feast day of Nuestra Señora de la Ascensión; dances

AUG   (Two weeks before Labor Day) Dances in patio of Palace of the Governors in Santa Fe, in conjunction with annual Indian Market sponsored by the Southwestern Association on Indian Affairs

AUG 28   San Agustín fiesta at Isleta

AUG   (Late August) Hopi snake dance—a solar observance; in even years at

---

*Since Isleta adopted its constitution, the ceremonial calendar has undergone various changes. One may see dances performed by either the Laguna group which dwells in the pueblo, or by the Isleta group. Dates should be checked annually.

Shipaulovi, Shungopavi, and Hotevila; in odd years at Mishongnovi and Walpi. Usually takes place about 4:00 p.m. Alternately, when snake dances are not held in a village, flute ceremonials are given. The dances are announced sixteen days before they are due to happen.

See note under June (late) or during July.

SEPT 1	Southern Ute fair
SEPT 2	Acoma feast day of San Estéban—corn dance atop mesa
SEPT 4	Isleta feast day, harvest dance
SEPT 8	Encinal (Laguna) harvest and social dances
SEPT 8	San Ildefonso, harvest dance*
SEPT 14-15	Jicarilla Apache celebration at Horse or Stone Lake
SEPT	(Mid-September, or earlier) Navajo Tribal Fair, Window Rock, Arizona—exhibits, horse races, rodeo, dances
SEPT 19	Laguna, feast day of San José; harvest dance and others; trading
SEPT 29	Taos, sundown dance—begins at sunset
SEPT 30	Taos, feast day of San Gerónimo—relay races (early) and pole climbing; dancing
SEPT	(Usually in September) Hopi *Maraüm*, women's social function
FALL	(Some time in fall) Fall Southern Ute Fair; rodeo; Northern Ute sundance
OCT	(1st week) Annual Navajo Fair at Shiprock, New Mexico
OCT 4	Nambé, feast day of San Francisco (Saint Francis); dancing
	At Magdalena, Sonora, Mexico, the Fiesta of Saint Francis of Assisi; hundreds of Papago, Pima, Yaqui, and Mayo Indians (who are affiliated with the Yaqui) converge there each year.
OCT	(Last Saturday and Sunday) Papago rodeo and fair at Sells, Arizona
OCT 31-NOV 2	On one of these days, ceremonies in most of the pueblos; gifts to the padres, and gifts to the dead placed on graves
OCT	(Usually in October) Hopi *Oáqol,* women's social function
NOV 1-2	In the San Xavier cemetery, near Tucson, hundreds of candles are lighted around the graves at night; this is true in all Papago cemeteries
NOV 12	Jémez and Tesuque, feast day of San Diego; dances
NOV	(Usually in November) Hopi *Wüwüchim*—tribal initiation ritual for all boys about 10-12 years

*Because so many San Ildefonso Indians work at Los Alamos, the ceremonies traditionally held at this time of the year have been shifted to the weekend closest to the old dates. The same situation prevails at San Juan, Santa Clara, and Tesuque with regard to dances. Check dates annually.

NOV   Colorado River tribes two-day rodeo at Parker, Arizona

NOV-DEC   (Some time in November or December) The *Shalako* at Zuñi; dancing in new houses and in house of the Koyemshi

Navaho reservation Nightway and Mountain Topway ceremonies

DEC 3   Ceremony at San Xavier in honor of Saint Francis Xavier

DEC 10-12 Fiesta of Tortuga Indians in honor of Our Lady of Guadalupe, near Las Cruces, New Mexico: processions and dancing

DEC 12   Guadalupe day at Isleta and Santo Domingo—gift throwing

DEC 12   Jémez *matachines;* Tesuque flag, deer, or buffalo dances

DEC 25   Taos deer or *matachines* dance (afternoon)

Christmas Day and two or three days following, dances at most of the pueblos

DEC 31   *New Year's Eve*, before midnight mass and dancing in church at Laguna, Sandía, San Felipe, Santo Domingo, and other pueblos

DEC   In the various Hopi villages, *Soyala*—winter solstice rites; opening of the katsina season, the purpose of which is to induce the sun to start on the first half of its journey. After this ceremony, other katsinas may appear at any time during the next six months.

POPULATION FIGURES
.... (1 January 1970)

PUEBLO INDIANS	*TANOAN (10,017)*	
(35,351)		

Tewa	*3,658*	*Keres, western*	7,947
Nambé	328	Acoma	2,861
Pojoaque	107	Laguna	5,086
San Ildefonso	358	*ZUÑIAN (5,640)*	
San Juan	1,487	*Zuñi*	
Santa Clara	1,119		*5,640*
Tesuque	259		
Tiwa, northern	*1,806*	*HOPI (6,019)*	
Picurís	163	*First Mesa*	*1,371*
Taos	1,623	Polacca	755
		Walpi	81
Tiwa, southern	*2,788*	Sitchumovi	335
Isleta	2,527	Hano (Tewa)	200
Sandía	261		
Guadalupe Indian Village	*	*Second Mesa*	*1,435*
		Shipaulovi	202
Towa	*1,765*	Mishongnovi	426
Jémez	1,765	Shungopavi	742
		Sun Light Mission	65
KERESAN (13,675)			
Keres, eastern	*5,728*	*Third Mesa*	*1,938*
Cóchiti	779	New Oraibi	720
San Felipe	1,632	Old Oraibi	180
Santa Ana	472	Bacabi	238
Santo Domingo	2,311	Hotevila	800
Zía	534		
		Moencopi	*1,019*
*Unknown		*Keams Canyon*	*256*

THE ATHABASCANS	*NAVAHO (126,267)*	*Tuba City Agency*	*23,043*
(ca. 140,100)	*Chinle Agency*	*21,150*	*APACHE (13,837)*
	Eastern Navaho Agency	*28,210*	*Jicarilla*	*1,742*
	Cañoncito	ca. 1,125		
	Checkerboard	ca. 24,785	*Mescalero*	*ca. 1,740*
	Puertocito (Alamo)	920		
	Ramah	1,380	Western Apache* (Ft.	
			Apache, San Carlos) ca. 10,355
	Fort Defiance Agency	*28,485*		
	Shiprock Agency	*25,379*	

*Arizona consus figures do *not* include off-reservation Indians.

82

THE UTE INDIANS (3,506)

UTE MOUNTAIN UTE

(Towaoc, Colo.)
(est. 1,146 enrolled)

SOUTHERN UTE

(Ignacio, Colo.) (760 enrolled)

NORTHERN UTE

(Ft. Duchesne, Utah) (1,600)

THE SOUTHERN PAIUTE (CA. 1,200)

KAIBAB PAIUTE

(over 100)

SHIVWITS PAIUTE

(150-200 enrolled)

CHEMEHUEVI

(now enrolled with Colo. River tribes) (ca. 600)

RANCHERIA PEOPLES (22,700)

COLORADO RIVER INDIAN TRIBES (4,451)

Chemehuevi, Mohave, Navaho, and Hopi together number 1,120 on reservation and 500 off reservation   1,620

Mohave at Fort Mohave (Parker, Ariz.)   511

Yuma (Quechan)—Ft. Yuma Reservation (1,007, plus 618 off reservation)   1,625

Cocopah (95 enrolled; includes ca. 300 in Mexico)   ca. 695

THE PAI (970)

Havasupai (eastern Pai)   ca. 270

Hualapai, or Walapai (western Pai)   ca. 685

Hualapai at Big Sandy, Ariz.   ca. 15

INDIANS OF THE SALT RIVER AGENCY (3,375)

Pima-Maricopa Community (1,700, plus 300 on nearby reservation)   2,000

Yavapai (Ft. McDowell
    Reservation)   ca. 300

Mohave-Apache (Ft. McDowell
    Reservation)   ca. 450

Yavapai Community   625
    Yavapai-Apache (Camp
        Verde, Ariz.)   ca. 200

    Tonto-Apache (Camp-
        Verde, Ariz.)   ca. 250

    Yavapai at Prescott   ca. 90
    "Payson Apache"   85

THE PIMANS (ca. 11,100)

*Pima (river people)—Gila
    River Community; a few
    Maricopa and Papago
    included   enrolled: ca. 5,300*

*Papago (desert people)—
    main reservation   ca. 5,800*

Maricopa—enumerated with Pima

THE CAHITANS (over 3,000)

Yaqui in Arizona   over 3,000

.........BIBLIOGRAPHY

Agogino, George A., and Michael L. Kunz (1971). "The Paleo Indian: Fact and Theory of Early Migrations to the New World," *The Indian Historian*, vol. 4, no. 1, Spring, pp. 21-26. The American Indian Historical Society. San Francisco.

Anderson, Jack (1969). "Papagos Living in Severe Poverty," Washington Merry-Go-Round, *Albuquerque Journal*, 15 November, pp. 3, 5.

_____ (1971). "Paiutes Nation's Most Deprived Tribe," *Albuquerque Journal*, 11 August.

Anonymous (1967). "Archeologists find Apache 'pueblos' near Las Vegas," *The New Mexican*, 23 April. Santa Fe.

_____ (1969a). "On Grand Canyon Floor. Havasupai Tribe to Get Houses," *Albuquerque Journal*, 15 June.

_____ (1969b). (On Navajo industries). *Arizona Republic*, 12 December. Phoenix.

_____ (1969c). "Indians: Squalor Amid Splendor," *Time*, 11 July. Chicago.

_____ (1969d). "White Mountain Apache Cattlemen," *New Mexico Stockman*, March, p. 49. Albuquerque.

_____ (1970a). "The Peyote Story," *Diné Baa Hane*, vol. 1, no. 11, August, pp. 12-13. Fort Defiance, Ariz.

_____ (1970b). "Ute Mountain Utes Ask Industrial Visits," *Albuquerque Journal*, 16 April.

_____ (1970c). "U.S. Government Honors Apache Tribes," *Albuquerque Journal*, 26 April: E-8.

_____ (1970d). "Indian Tribes Buy Part of Heritage," *The New Mexican*, 1 May. Santa Fe.

_____ (1970e). (On Hualapai Indians) *Albuquerque Journal*, 10 July.

_____ (1970f). "Zuni War Chief Dies," *The New Mexican*, 30 January. Santa Fe.

_____ (1970g). *Albuquerque Journal*, Action Line, 15 February.

_____ (1971a). "Arizona's 85 Payson Apaches Stump for Title to Tonto Land," *Albuquerque Journal*, 22 August: A-6 (Washington UPI)

_____ (1971b). "Luxury Complex Planned. Southern Ute Tribe Will Enter Tourist Business," *Albuquerque Journal*, 26 November.

_____(1971c). "Papago Indians Get Farm Grant," *Albuquerque Journal,* 25 December.

_____(1971d). "Indians Build $2 Million Resort," *The New Mexican,* 16 May. Santa Fe.

_____(1971e). "Master Potter of Maricopas Crushed to Death under Tree," *Arizona Republic,* 11 August, p. 21. Phoenix.

_____(1971f). "Ida Redbird Dies," *Newsletter,* The Heard Museum, September-October, Phoenix.

_____(1971g). "Fannin Asks Indian Aid," *The New Mexican,* 14 February. Santa Fe.

_____(1972). News Release, Window Rock, Ariz. 18 February.

_____(1973). *The New Mexican,* 5 August, p. B9. Santa Fe.

Arizona Commission of Indian Affairs (1971). *Tribal Directory.* 71 pp. Phoenix.

Arizona Writers' Project, WPA (1941). "The Apache," *Arizona Highways,* vol. xvii, no. 11, November, pp. 32-35, 42. Phoenix.

Bahti, Tom (1968). *Southwestern Indian Tribes.* KC Publications. Flagstaff.

Baldwin, Gordon C. (1965). *The Warrior Apaches.* Dale Stuart King. Tucson.

Ball, Eve (1970). *In The Days of Victorio.* Univ. of Arizona Press. Tucson.

Barnett, Franklin (1968). *Viola Jimulla: The Indian Chieftess.* Southwest Printers. Yuma, Ariz.

Bartel, Jon (1970). "First Indian High School Starts Classes at Ramah," *The Gallup Independent,* 12 August, p. 2B. Gallup, N. M.

Barton, Robert S. (1953). "The Lincoln Canes of the Pueblo Governors," *Lincoln Herald,* Winter, pp. 24-29.

Basehart, Harry W. (1967). "The Resource Holding Corp. Among the Mescalero Apache," *S. W. Journ. Anthro.,* vol. xxiii, pp. 277-291. Univ. of New Mexico Press. Albuquerque.

_____(1970). "Mescalero Apache Band Organization and Leadership," *S.W. Journ. Anthro.,* vol. xxvi, no. 1, pp. 87-104. Univ. of New Mexico Press. Albuquerque.

Berry, Norm (1971). "Light in the Desert," *Mountain Bell,* vol. ii, no. 2, Summer. Denver.

Bloom, Lansing B. (1940). "Who Discovered New Mexico?" *New Mexico Historical Review,* vol. xv, no. 2, April, pp. 101-132. Albuquerque.

Bolton, Herbert E. (1950). "Pageant in the Wilderness," *Utah Historical Quarterly*, vol. 18. Salt Lake City.

Brandon, William (1969). "American Indians: the Alien Americans," *The Progressive*, vol. xxxiii, no. 12, pp. 13-17. Madison, Wis.

———(1970a). "The American Indians: the Un-Americans," *The Progressive*, January, pp. 35-39. Madison, Wis.

———(1970b). "American Indians: the Real American Revolution," *The Progressive*, February, pp. 26-30. Madison, Wis.

Brennan, Bill (1966). "This is River Country," part one, The Colorado River Indian Reservation, pp. 9-11, 30-32; part two, Parker, Arizona—the Heart of the River Country, pp. 32-39 in *Arizona Highways*, vol. xlii, no. 2, February. Phoenix.

———(1967). "Parker—Power Boat Racing Capital of the Southwest," *The Parker-Lake Havasu Story,* pp. 16-17. Phoenix.

Breuninger, Evelyn P. (1970). "Debut of Mescalero Maidens," *Apache Scout,* vol. xvi, no. 5, June, pp. 1-5. Mescalero Reservation. Mescalero, N. M.

Brugge, David M. (1969).   "A Navajo History," unpublished manuscript. 22 pp.

Bunzel, Ruth L. (1932a). "Introduction to Zuñi Ceremonialism," 47th Ann. Rep., *Bureau of American Ethnology*, pp. 471-544. Govt. Printing Office, Washington, D. C.

———(1932b). Zuñi Katcinas: An Analytical Study," 47th Ann. Rep., *Bureau of American Ethnology*, pp. 843-903. Govt. Printing Office, Washington, D. C.

Carta Contenante le Royanne du Mexique et al Floride (n.d.) Old French map of early 1700s, in New Mexico State Record Center and Archives. Santa Fe.

Chaban, Ruth (1971). "The 1971 Annual Indian Market," *The Quarterly of the Southwestern Association on Indian Affairs, Inc.*, vol. vii, no. 2, Summer. Santa Fe.

Colton, Harold S. (1941). "Prehistoric Trade in the Southwest," *Scientific Monthly,* vol. 52, pp. 309-319. Amer. Assn. for the Advancement of Science. Washington, D. C.

Coues, Elliott (1900). *On the Trail of a Spanish Pioneer:* (the Diary and Itinerary of Francisco Garcés in his Travels Through Sonora, Arizona and California). 2 vols. Francis P. Harper. New York.

Coze, Paul (1952). "Of Clowns and Mudheads," *Arizona Highways,* vol. xxviii, no. 8, August, pp. 18-29. Phoenix.

_____(1971). "Living Spirits of Kachinam," *Arizona Highways,* Vol. xlvii, no. 6, June. Phoenix.

Cumming, Kendall (1967). Personal Letter, 21 April.

Davis, Irvine (1959). "Linguistic Clues to Northern Río Grande Prehistory," *El Palacio,* vol. 66, no. 3, June, pp. 73-83. Museum of N. M. Santa Fe.

Dittert, A.E., Jr. (1958). "Preliminary archaeological investigations in the Navajo project area of northwestern New Mexico,"

Papers in Anthro., no. 1, May, 25 pp., Museum of N. M. Press. Santa Fe.

_____(1959). "Culture Change in the Cebolleta Mesa Region, Central Western New Mexico," Doctoral dissertation, Univ. of Arizona (unpublished). Tucson.

_____(1967). Personal Information.

_____(1972). They came from the South," *Arizona Highways,* vol. xlviii, no. 1, January, pp. 34-39. Phoenix.

Dobyns, Henry F. and Robert C. Euler (1960). "A Brief History of the Northeastern Pai," *Plateau,* vol. 32, no. 3, January, pp. 49-56. Museum of No. Ariz. Flagstaff.

_____(1971). *The Havasupai People.* Indian Tribal Series. Phoenix.

Dobyns, Henry F., Paul H. Ezell, Alden W. Jones and Greta Ezell (1957). "Thematic Changes in Yuman Warfare: cultural stability and cultural change," *Proceedings,* Amer. Ethnol. Soc., pp. 46-71, annual spring meeting. Amer. Ethnol. Soc. Seattle.

Dockstader, Frederick J. (1954). *The Kachina and the White Man: A Study of the Influences of the White Culture on the Hopi Kachina Cult,* Bulletin no. 35. Cranbrook Institute of Science. Bloomfield Hills, Mich.

Douglas, F. H. (1931). "The Havasupai Indians," *Leaflet No. 33,* Denver Art Museum. 4 pp. Denver, Colo.

Drucker, Philip (1937). "Cultural Element Distributions: V" *Southern Calif. Anthropological Records,* vol. i, no. 1, Univ. of Calif. Press, Berkeley.

Dutton, Bertha P. (1963). *Sun Father's Way: The Kiva Murals of Kuana.* Univ. of N. M. Press. Albuquerque.

_____(1966). "Pots Pose Problems," *El Palacio,* vol. 73, no. 1, Spring, pp. 5-15. Museum of N. M. Press. Santa Fe.

_____(1972a) "The New Year of the Pueblo Indians of New Mexico," *El Palacio,* vol. 78, no. 1. Museum of N. M. Press.

_____(1972b). *Let's Explore: Indian Villages Past and Present.* Museum of N. M. press. 65 pp. Santa Fe.

Eddy, Frank W. (1965). "The Desert Culture of the Southwestern United States," Lecture at St. Michael's College (College of Santa Fe), 9 February (unpublished). Santa Fe.

_____(1966). "Prehistory in the Navajo Reservoir District, Northwestern New Mexico," *Papers in Anthro.*, no. 15, pt. I. Museum of N. M. Press. Santa Fe.

_____(1974). "Population dislocation in the Navaho reservoir district, New Mexico and Colorado," *Amer. Antiquity*, vol. 39, no. 1:75-84.

Eggan, Fred (1950). *Social Organization of the Western Pueblos.* Univ. of Chicago Press. Chicago.

Eklund, D. E. (1969). "Pendleton Blankets," *Arizona Highways,* vol. xlv, no. 8, August, p. 40. Phoenix.

Ellis, Florence (Hawley) (1964). "Archaeological History of Nambé Pueblo, 14th Century to Present," *American Antiquity,* vol. 30, no. 1, July, pp. 34-42. Soc. for Amer. Archaeology. Salt Lake City.

Emmitt, Robert (1954). *The Last War Trail – The Utes and the Settlement of Colorado.* Univ. of Oklahoma Press. Norman.

Euler, Robert C. (1961). "Aspects of Political Organization Among the Puertocito Navajo," *El Palacio*, vol. 68, no. 2, Summer, pp. 118-120. Museum of N.M. Santa Fe.

_____(1966). "Southern Paiute Ethnohistory," *Anthro. Papers.* no. 78, April. Univ. of Utah Press. Salt Lake City.

_____(1972a). *The Paiute People.* Indian Tribal Series. Phoenix.

_____(1972b). Personal Letter, 7 July.

Ezell, Greta S. and Paul H. Ezell (1970). "Background to Battle: Circumstances Relating to Death on the Gila, 1857," in *Troopers West: Military and Indian Affairs on the American Frontier,* pp. 169-186. Frontier Heritage Press. San Diego.

Faris, Chester E. (n.d.). "Pueblo Governors' Canes," Mimeographed report. 7 pp.

Fontana, B. L. (1967). Personal Letter, 6 January.

Fontana, B. L., Wm. J. Robinson, C. W. Cormack and E. E. Leavitt, Jr. (1962). *Papago Indian Pottery.* Univ. of Wash. Press. Seattle.

Forrest, Earle R. (1961). *The Snake Dance of the Hopi Indians.* Westernlore Press. Los Angeles.

Forrestal, Peter P. (transl.) and Cyprian J. Lynch (historical intro. and notes) (1954). *Benavides' Memorial of 1630.* Academy of Amer. Franciscan Hist. Washington, D. C.

Fort Mohave Tribal Council (California-Arizona-Nevada) (1970). *Letter and Resolution*, 27 October, 6 pp. Needles, Calif.

Fowler, Catherine S. (1971).   Personal Letter, 14 June.

Fowler, Don D. and Catherine S. Fowler (Eds.) (1971).   "Anthropology of the Numa: John Wesley Powell's manuscripts on the Numic Peoples of Western North America, 1868-1880," *Smithsonian Contributions to Anthro.*, No. 14, Smithsonian Institution. Washington, D. C.

Gabel, Norman E. (1949). *A Comparative Racial Study of the Papago*, Univ. of New Mexico Publications in Anthro., no. 4, Univ. of N. M. Press. Albuquerque.

Galvin, John (Transl. and Ed.) (1967). *A Record of Travels in Arizona and California, 1775-1776, Father Francisco Garcés.* John Howell Books. San Francisco.

Gerald, Rex E. (1958)   "Two Wickiups on the San Carlos Indian Reservation, Arizona," *The Kiva*, vol. 23, no. 3, February, pp. 5-11. Ariz. Arch. and Hist. Society. Tucson.

Gilliland, H. M. (1972). Personal Letter and data sheets. *Hopi Indian Agency*, 16 March. Keams Canyon, Ariz.

Gonzales, Clara (1969). *The Shalakos Are Coming.* Museum of N. M. Press. 13 pp. Santa Fe.

Goodwin, Grenville (1942). *The Social Organization of the Western Apache.* Univ. of Chicago Press. Chicago.

Graves, Howard (1970).   "Jobs, Tradition, Urbanization Key Navajo Race Factors," *Albuquerque Journal*, 24 August.

Gunnerson, James H. (1960).   "An Introduction to Plains Apache Archaeology—the Dismal River Aspect," *B. A. E. Anthro. Paper No. 58.* Washington, D. C.

_____(1969a). "Apache Archaeology in Northeastern New Mexico," *American Antiquity*, vol. 34, pp. 23-39. Soc. for Amer. Archaeology. Salt Lake City.

_____(1969b). "Archaeological Survey on and near Pecos National Monument—Preliminary Report," mimeographed report, pp. 1-9.

Gunnerson, James H. and Dolores A. (1970).   "Evidence of Apaches at Pecos," *El Palacio*, vol. 76, no. 3, pp. 1-6, Museum of N. M. Santa Fe.

_____(1971a). "Apachean Culture: A Study in Unity and Diversity," reprinted from *Apachean Culture History and Ethnology, Anthro. Papers, No. 21,* pp. 7-22. Univ. of Ariz, Tucson.

_____(1971b). "Apachean Culture History and Ethnology," *Anthro. Papers, No. 21,* 22 pp., Univ. of Ariz. Tucson.

Hackett, Charles Wilson (1937). *Historical Documents Relating to*

New Mexico, Nueva Vizcaya, and Approaches thereto, to 1773. 3 vols. Carnegie Institution. Washington, D. C.

Hanlon, C. J. (O. F. M.) (1972). "Papago Funeral Customs," *The Kiva,* vol. 37, no. 2, Winter, pp. 104-112. Ariz. Arch. and Hist. Society. Tucson.

Harrington, John P. (1940). "Southern Peripheral Athapaskawan Origins, Divisions, and Migrations," *Essays in Historical Anthropology of North America, Smithsonian Misc. Colls.,* vol. 100, pp. 503-532. Smithsonian Institution, Washington, D. C.

Hawley, Florence (1950). "Big Kivas, Little Kivas, and Moiety Houses in Historical Reconstruction," *S. W. Journal of Anthro.,* vol. 6, no. 3, Autumn, pp. 286-300. Univ. of N. M. Press. Albuquerque.

Hawley, Florence and Donovan Senter (1946). "Group-designed Behavior Patterns in Two Acculturating Groups," *S. W. Journal of Anthro.,* vol. 2, no. 2, pp. 133-151. Univ. of N. M. Press. Albuquerque.

Hayes, George (1971). Personal Information. Pojoaque, New Mexico, 18 November.

Hester, James J. (1962). "Early Navajo Migrations and Acculturation in the Southwest," *Papers in Anthro.* no. 6, 131 pp. Museum of N. M. Press. Santa Fe.

Hewett, E. L. and B. P. Dutton (1945). *The Pueblo Indian World.* Univ. of N. M. Press. Albuquerque.

Hill, W. W. (1940). "Some Aspects of Navajo Political Structure," *Plateau,* vol. 13, no. 2. Reprint, 6 pp. Museum of No. Ariz. Flagstaff.

Hodge, Frederick W. (Ed.) (1910). "Handbook of American Indians North of Mexico," *B. A. E. Bull. 30,* part two: p. 186. Smithsonian Institution. Washington, D. C.

Hoebel, E. Adamson (1958). *Man in the Primitive World.* McGraw-Hill Book Co. New York, London and Toronto.

Hoijer, Harry (1938). *Chiricahua and Mescalero Apache Texts.* Univ. of Chicago Press. Chicago.

―――(1956) "The Chronology of the Athapaskan Languages," *International Journal of American Linguistics,* vol. 22, no. 4, October, pp. 219-232. Baltimore.

Hoijer, Harry et al. (1963). "Studies in the Athapaskan Languages," *Publications in Linguistics,* University of California.

Hopi Reservation. (a mimeographed leaflet of information) issued by the Hopi Tribe. 13 pp. Keams Canyon, Ariz.

Houser, Nicholas P. (1972). "The Camp"—An Apache Community of Payson, Arizona," *The Kiva,* vol. 37, no. 2, Winter, pp. 65-71. Ariz. Arch. and Hist. Society. Tucson.

Hume, Bill (1970a). "Sandia Pueblo Adopts Best of Two Cultures," *Albuquerque Journal*, 9 August, p. D-1.

_____(1970b). "Prehistoric Site, Scenic Canyon Boost Santa Clara's Finances," *Albuquerque Journal*, 4 October, p. G-1.

____(1974). "The Havasupai Prisoners of Grand Canyon," *Indian Affairs,* No. 86 (Newsletter). March-April, pp. 1-2, 7. New York.

Huscher, B. H. and H. A. (1942). "Athapascan Migration via the Intermontane Region," *American Antiquity,* vol. 8, no. 1, pp. 80-88. Soc. for Amer. Archaeology. Menasha, Wis.

_____(1943). "The Hogan Builders of Colorado," *Colorado Archaeological Society.* Gunnison, Colo.

James, Harry C. (1956). *The Hopi Indians.* The Caxton Press. Caldwell, Idaho.

Johnston, Bernice (1970). *Speaking of Indians.* Univ. of Arizona Press. Tucson.

Kaut, Charles R. (1957). "The Western Apache Clan System: Its Origins and Development," *Publications in Anthro.,* no. 9, 85 pp. Univ. of New Mexico. Albuquerque.

Kelly, Dorothea S. (1950). "A Brief History of the Cocopa Indians of the Colorado River Delta," in *For the Dean,* pp. 159-169. Hohokam Museums Association and the Southwestern Monuments Association. Tucson, Arizona and Santa Fe, N. M.

Kelly, Isabel (1964). "Southern Paiute Ethnography," *Anthro. Papers,* No. 69. May. Univ. of Utah Press. Salt Lake City.

Kelly, William H. (1953). *Indians of the Southwest: A Survey of Indian Tribes and Indian Administration in Arizona.* 1st Ann. Rep. Bureau of Ethnic Research, Dept. Anthro., 129 pp. Tucson.

King, William S. (1967). Information from Salt River Indian Agency, Scottsdale, Arizona, 11 April, 3 pp.

Kluckhohn, Clyde and Dorothea Leighton (1962). *The Navajo.* Doubleday & Co., Inc. Garden City, N. Y.

Kluckhohn, Clyde and Leland C. Wyman (1940). "An Introduction to Navaho Chant Practice," *Memoirs,* no. 53, Amer. Anthro. Assn. Menasha, Wis.

Kurath, William and Edward H. Spicer (1947). "A Brief Introduction to Yaqui, a Native Language of Sonora," *Bulletin* (Social Science Bull. no. 15) Univ. of Ariz. Tucson.

Levy, Jerrold E. (1965). "Navajo Suicide," *Human Organization,* vol. 24. no. 4, pp. 308-318. Soc. for Applied Anthro. Ithaca, N. Y.

Levy, Jerrold E., Stephen J. Kunitz, and Michael Everett (1969). "Navajo Criminal Homicide," *S.W. Jrnl. of Anthro.*, vol. 25, no. 2, Summer, pp. 124-149. Univ. of N. M. Albuquerque.

Link, Martin A. (1968). (Introduction to) *Treaty between the United States of America and the Navajo Tribe of Indians*, KC Publications. Flagstaff, Ariz.

Lister, Robert H. (1958). "Archaeological Excavations in the Northern Sierra Madre Occidental, Chihuahua and Sonora, Mexico," *Univ. of Colorado Studies*, Series in Anthropology, no. 7. Boulder.

Lumholtz, Carl (1902). *Unknown Mexico*, 2 vols. Charles Scribner's Sons. New York.

McGregor, John C. (1951). *The Cohonina Culture of Northwestern Arizona*. Univ. of Illinois Press. Urbana, Illinois.

———(1967). *The Cohonina Culture of Mount Floyd, Arizona*. Univ. of Kentucky Press. Lexington, Ky.

McNitt, Frank (1970). "Fort Sumner: a Study in Origins," *New Mexico Historical Review*, April, pp. 101-115. Albuquerque.

Mangel, Charles (1970). "Sometimes We Feel We're Already Dead," *Look*, vol. 34, no. 11, 2 June, pp. 38-43. New York.

Martin, John (1972). Personal Letter. 3 April.

Matthews, Washington (1887). "The Mountain Chant: A Navajo Ceremony," Bureau American Ethnology, pp. 385-467. Washington, D. C.

———(1897). *Navaho Legends*. American Folklore Society. New York.

———(1902) "The Night Chant, a Navaho Ceremony," *Memoirs*, vol. vi, May. American Museum of Nat. Hist. New York.

Miller, Wick R. and C. G. Booth (1972). "The Place of Shoshoni among American Languages," *Introduction to Shoshoni Language Course Materials*. Aug. 9 pp. Owyhee, Nevada.

Montgomery, Ross Gordon, Watson Smith and J. O. Brew (1949). "Franciscan Awatovi, the Excavation and Conjectural Reconstruction of a 17th Century Spanish Mission Establishment at a Hopi Indian Town in Northeastern Arizona," *Papers, Peabody Mus. of Amer. Arch. and Ethnol.*, vol. xxxvi. Harvard Univ., Cambridge.

Montgomery, William (1970a). "Fruitland Mine, Plant Liked," *Albuquerque Journal*, 18 August, pp. A-1 and A-5.

———(1970b). "Black Mesa Coal Provides Indians Jobs," *Albu-*

querque Journal, 19 August, pp. A-1 and A-5.

———(1970c). "Navajo Generating Plant Now Building," *Albuquerque Journal*, 22 August, pp. A-1 and A-5.

———(1970d). "Water Key to Southwest's Growth," *Albuquerque Journal*, 26 August, pp. A-1 and A-5.

Morris, Clyde P. (1972). "Yavapai-Apache Family Organization in a Reservation Context," *Plateau*, vol. 44, no. 3, Winter, pp. 105-110. Museum of No. Ariz. Flagstaff.

Murray, Clyde A. (1969). "Homes in Flood Plain: CAP to Displace Indians," *The Arizona Republic*, 9 November, p. 24-B. Phoenix.

Moon, Sheila (1970). *A Magic Dwells*. Wesleyan Univ. Press. Middletown, Conn.

Nabokov, Peter (1969). "The Peyote Road," *The New York Times Magazine*, Sec. 6, 9 March, pp. 30-31, 129-132, 134.

Navajo Census Office (1970). Window Rock, Arizona.

Navajo Community College (n.d.). *Introducing the Navajo Community College*, 25 pp. brochure.

Navajo Tribal Museum (1968). *Historical Calendar of the Navajo People*. 15 July. Window Rock, Arizona.

New, Lloyd (1968). "Institute of American Indian Arts, Cultural Difference as the Basis for Creative Education," *Native American Arts*, no. 1. U. S. Dept. of the Interior, San Francisco. Washington, D. C.

Opler, Morris E. (1935). "The Concept of Supernatural Power Among the Chiricahua and Mescalero Apaches," *American Anthro.*, vol. 37, pp. 65-70. Menasha, Wis.

———(1938a). Ethnological Notes in *Chiricahua and Mescalero Apache Texts*, by Harry Hoijer. Univ. of Chicago Press. Chicago.

———(1938b). "Myths and Tales of the Jicarilla Apache Indians," *Memoirs* of the Amer. Folklore Society, vol. 31, 393 pp. New York.

———(1941). *An Apache Life-Way; The Economic, Social, and Religious Institutions of the Chiricahua Indians*. Univ. of Chicago Press. Chicago.

———(1942). "Myths and Tales of the Chiricahua Apache Indians," *Memoirs* of the Amer. Folklore Society, vol. xxxvii, 101 pp. New York.

———(1943). "Navaho Shamanistic Practice Among the Jicarilla Apache," *New Mexico Anthropologist*, vols. vi, vii, no. 1. Jan.-Mar., pp. 13-18. Univ. of Chicago Press.

Ortiz, Alfonso (1969). *The Tewa World.* Univ. of Chicago Press. Chicago and London.

Painter, Muriel Thayer and E. B. Sayles (1962). *Faith, Flowers and Fiestas.* Univ. of Arizona Press. Tucson.

Papago Indian Agency (1970). *Facts about the Papago Indian Reservation and the Papago People.* (Mimeographed.) 12 pp. Sells, Ariz.

Parsons, Elsie Clews (1925). *The Pueblo of Jemez.* Phillips Academy. Andover, Mass.

_____(1939). *Pueblo Indian Religion.* 2 vols. Univ. of Chicago Press. Chicago.

Powell, John W. (1891). "Indian Linguistic Families of America North of Mexico." Bureau American Ethnology, *7th Ann. Rep.* Washington, D. C.

Reed, Verner Z. (1896). "The Ute Bear Dance," *American Anthro.,* vol. ix, July, pp. 237-244. Menasha, Wis.

Reichard, Gladys A. (1963). *Navaho Religion,* Bollingen Series 18, Pantheon Books. New York

Richards, David (1970). "America's Silent Minority," *TWA Ambassador,* vol. 3, no. 5, pp. 7-12. St. Paul, Minn.

Robinson, A. E. (Bert) (1954). *The Basket Weavers of Arizona.* Univ. of N. M. Press. Albuquerque.

Sandoval, H. (1971). "Views on '*A Gunfight,*' " *The Jicarilla Chieftain,* 1 November. Dulce, New Mexico. (editorial)

Sapir, Edward (1929). "Central and North American Languages," in *The Encyclopaedia Britannica* (14th Ed.), vol. 5, pp. 139-141.

Schaafsma, Polly (1966). *Early Navaho Rock Paintings and Carvings.* Museum of Navaho Ceremonial Art, Inc. Santa Fe.

Schevill, Margaret Erwin (1947). *Beautiful on the Earth.* Hazel Dreis Editions. Santa Fe.

Schoenwetter, James and A. E. Dittert, Jr. (1968). "An Ecological Interpretation of Anasazi Settlement Patterns," in *Anthropological Archaeology in the Americas.* The Anthro. Society of Washington. pp. 41-61. Washington, D. C.

Schroeder, Albert H. (1963). "Navajo and Apache Relationships West of the Rio Grande," *El Palacio,* vol. 70, no. 3, Autumn, pp. 5-20. Museum of New Mexico. Santa Fe.

Schwartz, Douglas W. (1956). "The Havasupai 600 A.D.–1955 A.D.: A Short Culture History," *Plateau,* vol. 28, no. 4, April, pp. 77-84. Museum of No. Ariz. Flagstaff.

_____(1959). "Culture Area and Time Depth: the Four Worlds of the Havasupai," *American Anthro.,* vol. 61, no. 6, December, pp. 1060-1069. Menasha, Wis.

Shepardson, Mary (1963). "Navajo Ways in Government (a Study in Political Process)," *Memoir 96,* Amer. Anthro. Assn. vol. 65, no. 3, pt. 2, June. Menasha, Wis.

Smith, Anne (1965). *New Mexico Indians Today.* A report prepared as part of the N. M. State Resources Development Plan. Museum of N. M. June, 279 pp. Santa Fe.

_____(1966). *New Mexico Indians:* Economic, educational, and social problems. Museum of N. M., Research Records no. 1. 58 pp. Santa Fe.

_____(1968). *Indian Education in New Mexico.* Div. of Govt. Research, Institute for Social Research and Dev. Univ. of N. M., July, 49 pp. Albuquerque.

_____(1974). *Ethnography of the Northern Ute.* Museum of N. M. Press. Papers in Anthropology no. 17. 285 pp. Santa Fe.

Smith, Watson (1952). "Kiva Mural Decorations at Awatovi and Kawaika-a, with a Survey of Other Wall Paintings in the Pueblo Southwest," *Papers,* Peabody Mus. of Amer. Arch. and Ethnol., Harvard Univ., vol. xxxvii. Reports of the Awatovi Exped. Report no. 5. Cambridge.

_____(1971). "Painted Ceramics of the Western Mound at Awatovi," *Papers,* Peabody Mus. of Amer. Arch. and Ethnol., Harvard Univ., no. 38. Cambridge.

Sonnichsen, C. L. (1958). *The Mescalero Apaches.* Univ. of Oklahoma Press. Norman, Okla.

Southwestern Monuments Monthly Report, Supplement for November (1937). U. S. Dept. of Interior, Natl. Park Service. p. 396. Coolidge, Ariz.

Spencer, Katherine (1947). *Reflection of Social Life in the Navaho Origin Myth.* Univ. of N. M. Press. Albuquerque.

Spencer, Robert (1940). "A Preliminary Sketch of Keresan Grammar," Master's Thesis, Univ. of New Mexico (unpublished).

Spicer, Edward H. (1970). *Cycles of Conquest* (the impact of Spain, Mexico, and the United States on the Indians of the Southwest 1533-1960). Univ. of Ariz. Press. Tucson.

Spicer, Edward H., Phyllis Balastrero, and Ted DeGrazia (1971). "Yaqui Easter Ceremonial," *Arizona Highways,* vol. xlvii, no. 3, March, pp. 2-10, 11, 34, 45-47. Phoenix.

Spier, Leslie (1928). "Havasupai Ethnography," *Anthro. Papers,* Amer. Museum of Natural History, vol. 29, pt. 3:286. New York.

_____(1955). "Mohave Culture Items," *Bulletin 28,* Museum of Northern Arizona, Northern Arizona Society of Science and Art, Inc. Flagstaff.

Spinden, Herbert J. (Transl.)(1933). *Songs of the Tewa.* New York.

Stephen, Alexander M. (E. C. Parsons, Ed.) (1936). *Hopi Journal,* 2 vols., Columbia Univ. Contribs. to Anthro., vol. 23. New York.

Steward, Julian H. (1955). *Theory of Culture Change.* Univ. of Illinois Press. Urbana, Illinois.

Stewart, Kenneth M. (1967). "Chemehuevi Culture Changes." *Plateau,* vol. 40, no. 1, Summer, pp. 14-20. Museum of Northern Arizona. Flagstaff.

Strong, William Duncan (1927). "An Analysis of Southwestern Society," *American Anthropologist,* vol. 29, no. 1, Jan.-Mar. 1927. Menasha, Wis.

Swadish, Morris (1967). "Linguistic Classification in the Southwest," in *Studies in Southwestern Ethnolinguistics,* pp. 281-306. Mouton & Co. The Hague and Paris.

Swanton, John R. (1952) "The Indian Tribes of North America," Bur. of Amer. Ethnology, Smithsonian Inst., *Bull. 145.* Washington, D.C.

Taylor, Morris F. (1970). "Campaigns Against the Jicarilla Apache, 1855," *New Mexico Historical Review,* April, pp. 119-133. Albuquerque.

Thrapp, Dan L. (1967). "Christian Missions Bested: 45% of Navajos Accept Peyote-Oriented Church," *Los Angeles Times,* 17 August.

Trager, George L. (1969). "Navajo Mountain—Navaho Molehill?" *Newsletter,* Amer. Anthro. Assn., p. 2. Menasha, Wis.

Uintah and Ouray Agency (Ute) (1970). Letter, 3 September. Fort Duchesne, Utah.

Underhill, Ruth M. (1938a). "A Papago Calender Record," *Bull., Anthro. Series,* vol. 2, no. 5, 1 March, 64 pp. Albuquerque.

_____(1938b). *Singing for Power.* Univ. of Calif. Press. Berkeley.

_____(1940). *The Papago Indians of Arizona,* Sherman Pamphlets, no. 3, 63 pp. Education Division, U. S. Office of Indian Affairs.

Ute Mountain Ute Agency, Towaoc, Colorado (n.d.[a], 1969?). "The American Indians of Colorado," 5 pp. Mimeographed report.

_____(n.d.[b], 1969?). "A Brief History of the Colorado Utes," 3 pp. Mimeographed report.

_____(1970). Letter, 18 August.

Van Valkenburgh, Richard (1945). "The Government of the Navajos," *Ariz. Quarterly,* vol. 1, pp. 63-73. Univ. of Ariz. Press. Tucson.

Vestal, Paul A. (1952). "Ethnobotany of the Rimrock Navaho," *Papers.* Peabody Mus. of Amer. Arch. and Ethnol., vol. 40, no. 4. Harvard Univ. Cambridge.

Vogt, Evon Z. (1951). "Navaho Veterans—a Study of Changing Values," *Papers,* Peabody Mus. of Amer. Arch. and Ethnol., vol. xli, no. 1. Harvard Univ. Cambridge.

Waliczed, John (1970). "Navajo High School Opens Door at Home," *The New Mexican,* 6 September (from Gallup Independent for AP). Santa Fe.

Walker, George W. (1970). "Celebrating the Arrival of Dr. Charles H. Cook, after Whom Cook Training School is Named, at Sacaton, Arizona," *Indian Highways,* no. 134, December, pp. 4 and 6. Cook Christian Training School. Tempe, Ariz.

White, Leslie A. (1935). "The Pueblo of Santo Domingo, New Mexico," *Memoirs* of the Amer. Anthro. Assn., no. 43, pp. 1-210. Menasha, Wis.

Whitfield, Charles (1971). Personal Information, long distance phone call, 11 May.

Whiting, Alfred F. (1958). "Havasupai Characteristics in the Cohonina," *Plateau,* vol. 30, no. 30, January, pp. 55-60. Museum of No. Ariz. Flagstaff.

Whitman, William III (1947). "The Pueblo Indians of San Ildefonso," *Contribs. to Anthropology, Columbia Univ.* no. 34. New York.

Willey, Gordon R. (1966). *An Introduction to American Archaeology,* vol. I. Prentice-Hall, Inc. Englewood Cliffs, New Jersey.

Yazzie, Ethelou (Ed.) (1971). *Navajo History,* vol. I. Navajo Community College Press. Many Farms, Arizona.

Young, Robert W. (1961). "The Origin and Development of Navajo Tribal Government,". *The Navajo Yearbook,* Report no. viii, 1951-1961 a Decade of Progress, pp. 371-392. Navajo Agency. Window Rock, Ariz.

_____(1968). *The Role of the Navajo in the Southwestern Drama.* Robert W. Young and *The Gallup Independent.* Galley, N.M.

Young, Robert W., and William Morgan (1943). *The Navaho Language.* Education Div., U. S. Indian Service Phoenix.